Home Baking

Home Baking

Jacqueline Bellefontaine, Kathryn Hawkins,
Wendy Sweetser & Wendy Veale

Jb

JOHN BEAUFOY PUBLISHING

First published in the United Kingdom in 2012 by John Beaufoy Publishing,
11 Blenheim Court, 316 Woodstock Road, Oxford OX2 7NS, England
www.johnbeaufoy.com

10 9 8 7 6 5 4 3 2 1

ISBN 978-1-906780-82-1

Design: Glyn Bridgewater
Project management: Rosemary Wilkinson
Photography: St.John Asprey; Ian Garlick; Michael Prior; Stuart MacGregor
Illustrations: Stephen Dew

Printed and bound in Malaysia by Times Offset (M) Sdn. Bhd.

Photographs on pages 192–253 © Stuart MacGregor

RECIPE NOTES

• Where milk is used in a recipe,
this can be full-fat, semi-skimmed
or skimmed.
• All spoon measurements are level
unless otherwise stated
• Metric and imperial measurements
are not always exact equivalents, so
only follow one set of measurements
within each recipe.
• As individual ovens vary, the
cooking times given should only be
taken as a guide. For cakes, bake
for at least ¾ of the suggested
cooking time before opening the
oven door to test.
• Oven temperatures have been
given for conventional electric and
gas ovens. For fan ovens, use the
following equivalents:

Electricity °C	Electricity (fan) °C
110	90
120	100
130	110
140	120
150	130
160	140
170	150
180	160
190	170
200	180
220	200

Contents

Cookies

Makes 18
Prep time: 10 mins
Cook time: 12–15 mins

175 g/6 oz self-raising flour
75 g/3 oz butter, cut into cubes
75 g/3 oz caster sugar
1 egg, lightly beaten
6 tbsp maple syrup
approx. 18 pecan halves

Maple pecan cookies

1 Preheat the oven to 180°C/350°F/Gas 4.

2 Place the flour into a mixing bowl and add the butter. Rub in the butter with your fingertips until the mixture resembles fine breadcrumbs. Stir in the sugar. Add the egg and 4 tbsp of the maple syrup and mix until well combined.

3 Place small spoonfuls of the mixture onto baking sheets, allowing space for the cookies to spread. Push a pecan half into the centre of each one.

4 Bake for 12–15 minutes until golden. Brush the cookies with the remaining maple syrup whilst still hot, then transfer to a wire rack to cool completely.

Makes about 20
Prep time: 20 mins plus chilling
Cook time: 10–12 mins

50 g/2 oz butter, softened
50 g/2 oz caster sugar

1 egg
175 g/6 oz plain flour
a little milk
40 g/1½ oz toasted hazelnuts, finely chopped
2–3 tbsp lemon curd

Lemon and hazelnut slices

1 Beat together the butter and sugar until pale and fluffy. Beat in the egg, then beat in the flour, finally using your hands to bring the mixture together to form a soft dough. Divide the dough into 2 pieces and roll into logs about 25 cm/10 in long. Brush each log with a little milk.

2 Spread the chopped hazelnuts on a sheet of non-stick baking parchment. Place the logs on the nuts and roll to press lightly into the nuts to coat.

3 Place the logs on a lightly greased baking sheet. Flatten each log slightly. Using the handle of a wooden spoon, press a channel down the centre of each log. Fill the hollows with lemon curd. Chill for 30 minutes.

4 Preheat the oven to 190°C/375°F/Gas 5. Bake for 10–12 minutes until pale golden brown. Leave on the baking sheet until the lemon curd has set but the dough is still warm. Cut diagonally into slices and transfer to a wire rack to cool completely.

Makes about 18
Prep time: 15 mins
Cook time: 12–15 mins plus setting

100 g/4 oz butter, softened
100 g/4 oz caster sugar

1 egg, lightly beaten
75 g/3 oz plain chocolate chips
175 g/6 oz self-raising flour
3 tbsp cocoa powder
1/2 tsp chilli powder
25 g/1 oz white chocolate (optional)

Chilli choc cookies

1 Preheat the oven to 180°C/350°F/Gas 4. Lightly grease
2 or 3 baking sheets.

2 Beat the butter and sugar together until pale and fluffy,
then gradually beat in the egg. Stir in the chocolate chips.
Sift the flour, cocoa and chilli powder into the bowl and beat
together until combined to form a soft dough.

3 Place the dough on a large sheet of non-stick baking
parchment and roll out to a 30 x 20 cm/12 x 8 in rectangle.
If the dough is very soft, place another sheet of parchment on
top to make rolling easier. Cut the dough into 18 rectangles
and place on the prepared baking sheets.

4 Bake for 12–15 minutes. Allow to cool for 2–3 minutes
before transferring to a wire rack to cool completely.

5 To decorate if desired, melt the white chocolate in the
microwave or over a pan of hot water. Drizzle the white
chocolate back and forth over the cookies. Allow to set.

Makes about 16
Prep time: 15 mins
Cook time: 15–20 mins

100 g/4 oz butter
100 g/4 oz caster sugar
2 tbsp orange juice

grated zest of 1 orange
100 g/4 oz self-raising flour, sifted
100 g/4 oz rolled oats
50 g/2 oz dried cranberries, roughly chopped
25 g/1 oz chopped candied orange peel

Orange and cranberry biscuits

1 Preheat the oven to 180°C/350°F/Gas 4. Lightly grease 2 baking sheets.

2 Place the butter and sugar in a saucepan and heat gently, stirring until the butter melts and the sugar dissolves. Stir in the orange juice and zest. Remove from the heat and beat in the remaining ingredients.

3 Place dessertspoonfuls of the mixture on the baking sheets allowing space for the mixture to spread a little.

4 Bake for 15–20 minutes. Allow to cool for a minute, then transfer to a wire rack to cool completely.

Makes about 24
Prep time: 20 mins
Cook time: 10–12 mins plus setting

150 g/5 oz butter, softened
175 g/6 oz caster sugar
3 tbsp lime juice
grated zest of 1/2 lime

50 g/2 oz desiccated coconut
225 g/8 oz self-raising flour

ICING
150 g/5 oz icing sugar
1–2 tablespoons lime juice
grated zest of 1/2 lime

Lime and coconut biscuits

1 Preheat the oven to 180°C/350°F/Gas 4. Lightly grease 2 baking sheets.

2 Beat together the butter and sugar until pale and fluffy. Beat in the lime juice, zest and coconut. Add the flour and beat into the coconut mixture.

3 Place rounded dessertspoonfuls of the mixture well spaced on the baking sheet. Bake for 10–12 minutes or until golden. Allow to cool on the baking sheet for 2–3 minutes, then transfer to a wire rack to cool completely.

4 Sift the icing sugar into a bowl and stir in the lime juice and zest to form a smooth icing. Spread over the biscuits. Allow to dry for 1–2 hours or until the icing sets. Store in an airtight container for up to 5 days.

VARIATION
If time is short omit the icing, the cookies are still delicious!

Makes 16
Prep time: 15 mins
Cook time: 15–20 mins

125 g/4¹/₂ oz granulated sugar
1 tbsp dried lavender flowers

225 g/8 oz butter
225 g/8 oz plain flour
125 g/4¹/₂ oz ground rice
or semolina
caster sugar, to sprinkle (optional)

Lavender shortbreads

1 Place the sugar and lavender in a food processor and whiz for about 10 seconds. Add the butter and process until pale and fluffy. Add the flour and ground rice or semolina and whiz briefly until the dough begins to come together.

2 Tip out onto a work surface and continue bringing the mixture together to form a soft dough with your hands. Divide the dough into two. Form each piece into a ball, then roll out to form an 18 cm/7 in circle. Transfer to a baking sheet.

3 Press a fork into the edge of the circles to make a crinkled border and prick all over the surface. Mark each into 8 wedges, then chill for 30 minutes.

4 Preheat the oven to 190°C/375°F/Gas 5. Bake for 15–20 minutes until pale golden. Sprinkle with caster sugar if desired, then transfer to a wire rack to cool completely.

TIP

If you cannot find dried lavender, substitute the same amount of fresh, chopped rosemary for a similar scented biscuit.

Makes about 15
Prep time: 15 mins plus chilling
Cook time: 15–18 mins

100 g/4 oz butter, softened
50 g/2 oz icing sugar
$^1/_2$ tsp vanilla essence
175 g/6 oz plain flour
a little milk, if needed
fruit jam of your choice

Thumbprint cookies

1 Beat the butter and sugar until pale and fluffy, then beat in the vanilla essence. Gradually beat in the flour, bringing the mixture together to form a soft dough with your hands as you add the last of the flour. Add a little milk or water if the mixture is too dry.

2 Lightly dust your hands with flour and roll the dough into small balls about the size of a small walnut. Arranged well spaced on a baking sheet. Flatten slightly, then, using your thumb, make a deep hole in the centre of each cookie. Chill for 30 minutes.

3 Preheat the oven to 180°C/350°F/Gas 4. Bake for 10 minutes, then fill each hole with a little jam and return to the oven for 5–8 minutes until pale golden. Allow to cool on the sheet for a few minutes before transferring to a wire rack to cool completely.

VARIATION

For a chocolate thumbprint cookie: bake the cookies for 15 minutes until golden. Meanwhile, melt 50g/2 oz plain chocolate with 25 g/1 oz butter in a microwave or in a bowl over a pan of hot water. Beat in 25 g/1 oz icing sugar. Once the cookies are baked, spoon or pipe the melted chocolate into the centre of the cookies and allow to set.

Makes about 20
Prep time: 20 mins
Cook time: 15–20 mins

100 g/4 oz chopped toasted hazelnuts
2 medium egg whites
225 g/8 oz caster sugar
1 tsp cornflour
about 20 whole hazelnuts, to decorate

Hazelnut macaroons

1 Preheat the oven to 170°C/325°F/Gas 3. Line 2 baking sheets with non-stick baking parchment.

2 Place the hazelnuts in a grinder and whiz until very finely chopped. Put the egg whites in a large mixing bowl and whisk until standing in soft peaks. Gradually add half the sugar and whisk until combined and stiff peaks are formed.

3 Carefully fold in the remaining sugar, ground hazelnuts and cornflour. Place spoonfuls of the mixture well spaced on the baking sheets and press a whole hazelnut into the centre of each.

4 Cook for about 15–20 minutes until the macaroons are pale golden and can be easily removed from the paper.

TIP
Dip the base of the macaroon into melted chocolate for a special treat.

Makes about 15 small cookies
Prep time: 15 mins
Cook time: 12 – 15 mins plus setting

grated zest of 1 orange
8 large basil leaves, chopped
175 g/6 oz plain flour

50 g/2 oz butter, softened
50 g/2 oz caster sugar
2 tbsp orange juice

ICING
50 g/2 oz icing sugar
2 tsp orange juice

Orange and basil cookies

1 Preheat the oven to 180°C/350°F/Gas 4.

2 Place the butter and sugar in a mixing bowl and beat until pale and fluffy. Beat in the orange juice, zest and basil. Add the flour and beat until combined using your hands to finish bringing the mixture together.

3 Roll walnut-sized pieces of the dough into balls using lightly floured hands. Place on baking sheets, flatten slightly and bake for 12–15 minutes until pale golden. Allow to cool for a couple of minutes before transferring to a wire rack to cool completely.

4 Sift the icing sugar into a bowl and stir in the orange juice to form a smooth icing. Spread over the biscuits. Allow to dry for 1–2 hours or until the icing sets.

VARIATION
Add 25 g/1 oz candied orange peel or mixed chopped peel.

Makes about 20
Prep time: 20 mins
Cook time: 12 mins plus setting

100 g/4 oz butter, softened
100 g/4 oz caster sugar
2 tbsp instant coffee
4 tbsp boiling water
225 g/8 oz plain flour
50 g/2 oz ground rice

FILLING
50 g/2 oz unsalted butter
175 g/6 oz icing sugar
2 tsp milk
2 tsp vanilla essence

ICING
100 g/4 oz icing sugar
1/2 tsp instant coffee
drinking chocolate or cocoa powder, to dust

Cappuccino creams

1 Preheat the oven to 180°C/350°F/Gas 4.

2 Beat together the butter and sugar until light and fluffy. Dissolve the coffee in the boiling water, then beat in. Add the flour and ground rice and mix to form a firm dough.

3 Roll out the dough on a lightly floured surface to about 3 mm/1/8 in thick, then cut into 5 cm/2 in rounds with a cookie cutter. Place on baking sheets. Repeat until all the dough is used, re-rolling as necessary.

4 Bake for 12 minutes until golden. Allow to cool for a few minutes before transferring to a wire rack to cool completely.

5 To make the filling, beat the butter until fluffy, then gradually beat in the icing sugar, milk and vanilla. Use to sandwich the biscuits together in pairs.

6 To make the icing, sift the sugar into a bowl. Dissolve the coffee in 1 tablespoon of boiling water and stir into the icing sugar until smooth. Spread over the cookies and allow to set. Dust with a little drinking chocolate or cocoa powder.

Makes about 20–40 depending on size of cutters used
Prep time: 30 mins
Cook time: 10–12 mins plus setting

100 g/4 oz butter, softened
100 g/4 oz light muscovado sugar
225 g/8 oz plain flour
1 tbsp golden syrup

2 tbsp milk
2 tsp ground ginger (optional)

TO DECORATE
150 g/5 oz icing sugar
approx. 4 tsp tbsp water
food colouring and sprinkles (optional)

Iced Christmas cookies

1 Preheat the oven to 190°C/375°F/Gas 5. Grease 2 baking sheets.

2 Place the butter and sugar in a mixing bowl and beat until light and fluffy. Add the remaining ingredients and mix to form a soft dough.

3 Roll out the dough to 5 mm/¼ in thick and cut out different shapes using cookie cutters. Place on the baking sheets and bake for 10–12 minutes until crisp and golden.

4 Allow to cool on the baking sheets for 2–3 minutes, then transfer to a wire rack to cool completely.

5 To decorate, sift the icing sugar into a bowl, stir in enough water and mix to form a smooth icing. Colour the icing, if desired, with a few drops of food colouring. Spread or pipe over the biscuits and add sprinkles if desired. Allow to dry for 1–2 hours or until the icing sets. Store in an airtight container for up to 2 weeks.

TIP
If you want to hang the cookies on the tree make a hole in each cookie with a skewer before baking. Tie onto the tree with ribbon threaded through the hole.

Makes about 36
Prep time: 20 mins plus chilling
Cook time: 10–12 mins

150 g/5 oz butter, softened
75 g/3 oz caster sugar

1 tsp vanilla essence
5 tbsp double cream
250 g/9 oz plain flour
4 tbsp demerara sugar
1 tbsp ground cinnamon

Cinnamon twirls

1 Place the butter and sugar in a mixing bowl and beat until pale and fluffy. Beat in the vanilla essence and 3 tbsp of the double cream. Add the flour and mix to a smooth soft dough.

2 Roll out the dough on a sheet of non-stick baking parchment to form a rectangle about 30 x 20 cm/12 x 8 in. Brush the remaining cream over the surface of the dough. Mix together the demerara sugar and cinnamon, then sprinkle over the cream. Roll up from the long side like a Swiss roll. Cover and chill for 30 minutes.

3 Preheat the oven to 180°C/350°F/Gas 4. Cut the dough into 5 mm/¼ in slices and place well spaced on baking sheets.

4 Bake for 10–12 minutes until crisp. Cool for 2–3 minutes on the baking sheets, then transfer to a wire rack to cool completely.

Makes about 24
Prep time: 30 mins
Cook time: 15–20 mins plus setting

1 tbsp instant coffee
2 tbsp milk

175 g/6 oz butter, softened
50 g/2 oz caster sugar
1 egg yolk
175 g/6 oz plain flour
approx. 24 walnut halves
150 g/5 oz milk or plain chocolate

Walnut whirls

1 Preheat the oven to 170°C/325°F/Gas 3. Grease 2 baking sheets.

2 Place the coffee in a small pan with the milk and heat gently, stirring until the coffee dissolves. In a mixing bowl beat together the butter and sugar until light and fluffy. Beat in the egg yolk, then the coffee mixture. Stir in the flour to form a smooth thick paste.

3 Spoon into a piping bag fitted with a large star nozzle and pipe rosettes measuring about 5 cm/2 in across onto the baking sheets. Press a walnut half gently into the centre of each.

4 Bake for 15–20 minutes or until pale golden. Allow to cool on the baking sheets for 2–3 minutes, then transfer to a wire rack to cool completely.

5 Melt the chocolate in a bowl set over a pan of gently simmering hot water or in the microwave. Place the cookies on a sheet lined with baking parchment and drizzle the chocolate over them, then leave in a cool place until set.

VARIATION
Omit the coffee and replace with 2 tsp vanilla essence instead.

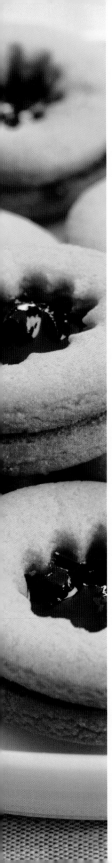

Makes about 24
Prep time: 25 mins
Cook time: 8–10 mins

75 g/3 oz butter, softened
75 g/3 oz caster sugar
100 g/4 oz smooth peanut butter
3 tbsp golden syrup
175 g/6 oz self-raising flour
fruit jam of your choice

Peanut jelly dodgers

1 Preheat the oven to 180°C/350°F/Gas 4.

2 Beat the butter and sugar together until pale and fluffy. Add the peanut butter and golden syrup, beating until well combined. Add the flour and work into the mixture to form a soft dough. Knead lightly.

3 Roll out the dough 5 mm/¼ in thick and cut out cookies using a 5 cm/2 in round cutter. Cut out the centre of half the cookies using a small round cutter. Re-roll these centre cut-outs to make further cookies. Place on baking sheets, with a little space around each. Bake for 8–10 minutes, until pale golden. Allow to cool on the sheets for a few minutes before transferring to a wire rack to cool completely.

4 Spread a little jam over the whole circles and place the rings on top.

Makes about 20
Prep time: 15 mins
Cook time: 12–15 mins

100 g/4 oz butter, softened
50 g/2 oz caster sugar

2 tbsp milk
75 g/3 oz glacé cherries, chopped
50 g/2 oz almonds, chopped
175 g/6 oz self-raising flour
75 g/3 oz marzipan

Cherry marzipan bites

1 Preheat the oven to 180°C/350°F/Gas 4.

2 Place the butter and sugar in a mixing bowl and beat until
pale and fluffy, then beat in the milk. Add the cherries,
almonds and flour and mix together to form a soft dough.

3 With lightly floured hands, break off small walnut-sized
pieces of the dough and roll into balls. Place on a baking
sheet allowing space for the cookies to spread and flatten with
a palette knife.

4 Grate the marzipan coarsely and sprinkle a little over
each cookie.

5 Bake for about 12–15 minutes until pale golden. Transfer
to a wire rack to cool completely.

Makes about 20
Prep time: 15 mins
Cook time: 10–12 mins

225 g/8 oz plain flour
1 tsp baking powder
1 tsp allspice

1/2 tsp ground cinnamon
1/2 tsp ground nutmeg
125 ml/41/2 fl oz sunflower oil
1 egg
150 g/5 oz full-flavoured clear honey

Honey and spice cookies

1 Preheat the oven to 190°C/375°F/Gas 5. Lightly grease
2 baking sheets.

2 Place the flour, baking powder and spices in a mixing
bowl and stir to combine. In another bowl, beat together
the oil and the egg, then pour into the centre of the dry
ingredients. Add the honey. Mix well.

3 Place spoonfuls of the mixture onto the baking sheets
allowing a little space for them to spread.

4 Bake for 10–12 minutes until golden. Allow to cool for
a few minutes on the baking sheets before transferring to
a wire rack to cool completely.

TIP
Suitable for a dairy-free
diet. You can replace the
spices listed with 2 tsp of
mixed spice.

Makes about 40
Prep time: 15 mins plus chilling
Cook time: 8–10 mins

175 g/6 oz butter, softened
75 g/3 oz light muscovado sugar

1 egg yolk
grated zest of 1/2 lemon
2 tbsp lemon juice
1 tbsp poppy seeds
225 g/8 oz plain flour

Lemon poppy seed cookies

1 Place the butter and sugar in a bowl and beat together until pale and fluffy. Beat in the egg yolk, lemon zest and juice. Mix the poppy seeds with the flour, then beat into the butter mixture to form a soft dough.

2 Shape into a long log about 5 cm/2 in thick. Wrap the log in a sheet of non-stick baking parchment and chill until required.

3 Preheat the oven to 190°C/375°F/Gas 5. Cut 5 mm/1/4 in thick slices from the log and place on baking sheets. Leave enough space for the cookies to spread.

4 Bake for 8–10 minutes until just firm. Allow to cool on the baking sheet for a few minutes before transferring to a wire rack to cool completely.

TIP
The uncooked biscuit log can be stored in the fridge for up to 1 week or place in a polythene bag and freeze for up to 2 months.

Makes about 18
Prep time: 15 mins
Cook time: 10–15 mins

100 g/4 oz light muscovado sugar
100 g/4 oz sunflower margarine
175 g/6 oz rolled oats

50 g/2 oz plain wholemeal flour
1 piece stem ginger in syrup, chopped plus
2 tbsp of the ginger syrup from the jar
1 egg

Ginger oat cookies

1 Preheat the oven to 180°C/350°F/Gas 4. Lightly grease 2 baking sheets.

2 Place the sugar and margarine in a saucepan and heat gently, stirring until combined. Place all the remaining ingredients, except the egg, in a large mixing bowl. Beat in the sugar mixture, then add the egg and beat until all the ingredients are well combined.

3 Place rounded tablespoonfuls of the mixture onto the baking sheets. Flatten slightly with the back of the spoon.

4 Bake for 10–15 minutes until golden. Allow to cool on the baking sheet for a few minutes before transferring to a wire rack to cool completely.

TIP
Suitable for a dairy-free diet. Oats and wholemeal flour are complex carbohydrates that release energy slowly helping you to feel fuller for longer.

Makes 16–20
Prep time: 15 mins
Cook time: 20–25 mins

225 g/8 oz butter
150 g/5 oz dark or light muscovado sugar

2 tbsp barley malt syrup or golden syrup
500 g/1lb 2 oz rolled oats
1 Granny Smith apple, peeled, cored and chopped
50 g/2 oz dried figs, chopped

Fruity flapjacks

1 Preheat the oven to 180°C/350°F/Gas 4. Lightly grease a 30 x 20 cm/12 x 8 in square, shallow cake tin.

2 Place the butter, sugar and syrup in a small saucepan and heat gently, stirring until combined. Place the oats in a mixing bowl and stir in the apple and figs. Make a well in the centre and pour in the butter and sugar mixture. Beat until well combined.

3 Pour into the cake tin and level the surface. Bake for 20–25 minutes. Allow to cool for 5 minutes in the tin, then cut into pieces whilst still warm and transfer to a wire rack to cool completely.

TIP
Barley malt syrup is available from health food shops and contains trace elements and B vitamins.

Makes about 16
Prep time: 25 mins
Cook time: 8–10 mins

100 g/4 oz butter, softened
100 g/4 oz icing sugar
1 egg, lightly beaten
grated zest of 1/2 orange
2 tbsp orange juice

150 g/5 oz plain flour
3 tbsp cocoa powder

FILLING
50 g/2 oz unsalted butter
grated zest of 1/2 orange
100 g/4 oz icing sugar
1 tbsp orange juice

Chocolate orange creams

1 Preheat the oven to 200°C/400°F/Gas 6. Line 2 or 3 baking sheets with non-stick baking parchment.

2 Beat the butter and sugar together until light and fluffy, then gradually beat in the egg. Beat in the orange zest and juice. Sift in the flour and cocoa powder together and beat well.

3 Place the mixture in a piping bag fitted with a large star nozzle. Pipe spirals onto the baking sheets about 3 cm/1¼ in wide, allowing plenty of space for the cookies to spread.

4 Bake for 8–10 minutes. Allow to cool on the baking sheets for a few minutes before transferring to a wire rack to cool completely.

5 For the filling, beat the butter until soft, then beat in the orange zest and gradually beat in the icing sugar. Finally beat in the orange juice. Use to sandwich two biscuits together. Store in a cool place and eat within 2 days.

Makes about 38
Prep time: 15 mins plus chilling
Cook time: 8–10 mins

175 g/6 oz butter, softened
100 g/4 oz light muscovado sugar
75 g/3 oz walnuts, very finely
chopped

1 tsp dried rosemary or 2 tsp
chopped fresh rosemary
175 g/6 oz plain flour
1 tsp baking powder
50 g/2 oz plain wholemeal flour

Walnut and rosemary cookies

1 Place the butter and sugar in a bowl and beat together
until pale and fluffy. Add the walnuts and rosemary and mix
to combine. Sift the plain flour and baking powder into
the bowl, then add the wholemeal flour and mix to form a
soft dough.

2 Shape into a long log about 5 cm/2 in thick. Wrap the log
in a sheet of non-stick baking parchment and chill until
required.

3 Preheat the oven to 190°C/375°F/Gas 5. Cut 5 mm/$^{1}/_{4}$ in
thick slices from the log and place on baking sheets, leaving
enough space between for the cookies to spread.

4 Bake for 8–10 minutes until just firm. Allow to cool on
the baking sheets for a few minutes before transferring to a
wire rack to cool completely.

TIP
Walnuts are a good
source of Vitamin E
and essential oils.

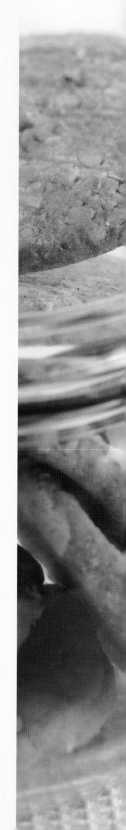

Makes about 20
Prep time: 20 mins plus cooling and chilling
Cook time: 10 – 12 mins

120 g/4½ oz unsalted butter
75 g/3 oz caster sugar
1 tsp vanilla essence
150 g/5 oz plain flour

Swedish butter cookies

1 Place the butter in a heavy-based saucepan and heat gently until it melts, then continue to cook until the butter turns a pale golden brown colour. Take care not to let it burn. Carefully pour the butter into a mixing bowl leaving behind the residue. Allow to cool and solidify.

2 Add the sugar to the cooled butter and beat until pale and fluffy. Beat in the vanilla, then beat in the flour and mix to form a firm dough. Form into a thick log and wrap in non-stick baking parchment. Chill for 30 minutes.

3 Preheat the oven to 190°C/375°F/Gas 5.

4 Cut the log into 3 mm/⅛ in thick slices and place on baking sheets. When you slice them, gently push the edges to form a round and they will re-form as they cook. Don't worry if the cookie cracks slightly. Bake for 10–12 minutes until pale golden. Allow to cool on the baking sheets for a few minutes before transferring to a wire rack to cool completely.

Makes about 18 large cookies
Prep time: 15 mins
Cook time: 10–12 mins

50 g/2 oz plain chocolate
50 g/2 oz white chocolate

50 g/2 oz milk chocolate
150 g/5 oz butter, softened
150 g/5 oz caster sugar
1 egg
1 tsp vanilla extract
200 g/7 oz self-raising flour

Triple choc chip cookies

1 Preheat the oven to 190°C/375°F/Gas 5. Lightly grease 2 baking sheets.

2 Chop all the chocolate into small chunks. Beat the butter and sugar together until pale and fluffy. Beat in the egg and vanilla extract. Stir in the chocolate. Sift the flour and beat into the mixture, until well combined.

3 Place round tablespoons of the mixture onto the baking sheets leaving plenty of space around each one. Shape each mound into a round and flatten slightly with the back of a spoon.

4 Bake for 10–12 minutes until golden. Allow to cool on the baking sheets for a few minutes before transferring to a wire rack to cool completely.

TIP
The irregular chunks of chocolate make these biscuits taste more 'homemade' but you can use ready-made chocolate chips if you prefer.

Makes about 18
Prep time: 25 mins
Cook time: 15–20 mins

225 g/8 oz butter, softened
50 g/2 oz icing sugar
1 tsp vanilla essence
225 g/8 oz plain flour
25 g/1 oz cornflour

Viennese shells

1 Preheat the oven to 170°C/325°F/Gas 3.

2 Beat together the butter and sugar until pale and fluffy.
Beat in the vanilla essence. Sift together the flour and
cornflour and beat into the mixture. Place the mixture in a
large piping bag fitted with a star nozzle.

3 Pipe small shells onto baking sheets.

4 Bake for 15–20 minutes or until pale golden. Allow to
cool on the baking sheets for 2–3 minutes, then transfer to a
wire rack to cool completely.

VARIATIONS
CHOCOLATE SHELLS: Melt about 150 g/5 oz milk or
plain chocolate in the microwave or in a bowl over a pan of
hot water. Half-dip each cooked shell in the melted
chocolate. Place on sheets of non-stick baking parchment
and allow to set.
CHERRY SHELLS: Decorate some or all of the shells by
pressing a half glacé cherry into the cookie before baking.

Makes about 30
Prep time: 20 mins
Cook time: 8–10 mins

175 g/6 oz butter, softened
225 g/8 oz caster sugar
1 large egg, lightly beaten
1 tsp vanilla essence

275 g/10 oz plain flour
1 tsp cream of tartar
1/2 tsp bicarbonate of soda

TO COMPLETE
1 tbsp caster sugar
2 tsp ground cinnamon

Snicker doodles

1 Preheat the oven to 200°C/400°F/Gas 6. Lightly grease
2 or 3 baking sheets.

2 Beat the butter and sugar together until pale and fluffy.
Gradually beat in the egg and vanilla essence. Sieve the
flour, cream of tartar and bicarbonate of soda together and
beat into the butter and sugar mixture to form a soft dough.

3 Mix the sugar and cinnamon together and place in a
shallow dish. With lightly floured hands, break off pieces of
the dough about the size of a small walnut and roll into a
ball. Roll each ball in the cinnamon mixture and place on
the baking sheets allowing space for the cookies to spread.

4 Bake for about 8–10 minutes until pale golden. Transfer
to a wire rack to cool completely.

TIP
Traditionally made
with cream of tartar
and bicarbonate
of soda, you can
replace these with
1 tsp baking
powder.

Makes about 24
Prep time: 20 mins
Cook time: 10–12 mins plus setting

50 g/2 oz butter
75 g/3 oz caster sugar
2 tbsp double cream

1 tbsp plain flour
50 g/2 oz sultanas
50 g/2 oz glacé cherries, chopped
25 g/1 oz crystallized ginger, chopped
100 g/4 oz flaked almonds
100 g/4 oz milk or plain chocolate

Florentines

1 Preheat the oven to 180°C/350°F/Gas 4. Line 2 baking sheets with non-stick baking parchment.

2 Place the butter and sugar in a small pan and heat gently until the butter has melted and the sugar dissolved. Remove from the heat and stir in the cream. Stir in the flour, sultanas, cherries, ginger and almonds until well mixed.

3 Place dessertspoonfuls of the mixture onto the baking sheets allowing plenty of space for the biscuits to spread. Bake for 10–12 minutes until pale golden. While the cookies are still hot use a greased circular cookie cutter to pull the edges of the cookies in to form neat circles. Take care not to touch the mixture as it will be very hot. Allow to cool completely before removing from the sheet.

4 Place the chocolate in a bowl over a pan of hot water until melted. Allow to cool, then spread onto the backs of the Florentines. Use a fork to mark squiggles in the chocolate and allow to set.

Makes about 24
Prep time: 15 mins
Cook time: 8–10 mins

100 g/4 oz self-raising flour
100 g/4 oz rolled oats

75 g/3 oz desiccated coconut
100 g/4 oz caster sugar
150 g/5 oz butter
1 tbsp golden syrup
1 tsp bicarbonate of soda
2 tbsp boiling water

Anzac biscuits

1 Preheat the oven to 180°C/350°F/Gas 4. Lightly grease
2 or 3 baking sheets.

2 Place the flour in a mixing bowl with the oats, coconut
and sugar and stir to combine.

3 Melt the butter with the golden syrup in a small saucepan.
Dissolve the bicarbonate of soda in the boiling water and add
to the pan. Pour over the dry ingredients and mix well.

4 Place spoonfuls of the mixture onto the baking sheets,
well spaced to allow the biscuits to spread.

5 Bake for 8–10 minutes until golden. Allow to cool for a
few minutes on the baking sheets before transferring to a
wire rack to cool completely.

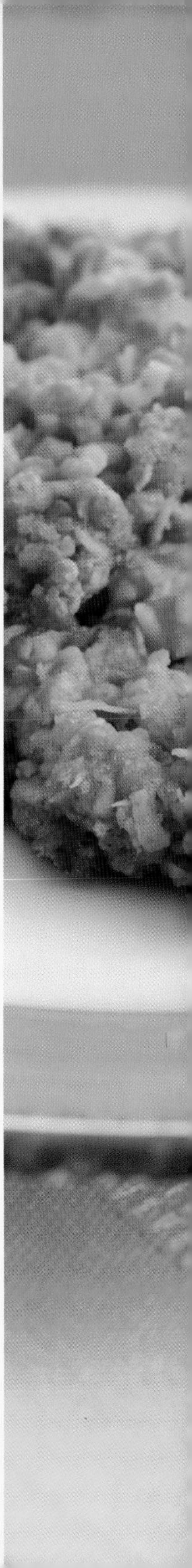

Makes about 16
Prep time: 15 mins
Cook time: 20 mins

175 g/6 oz self-raising flour
100 g/4 oz butter
75 g/3 oz caster sugar

2 tsp ground cinnamon
1 egg, separated
2 tbsp milk
40 g/1½ oz flaked almonds
1 tbsp natural sugar crystals or granulated sugar

Dutch Jan Hagel cookies

1 Preheat the oven to 180°C/350°F/Gas 4. Grease a shallow baking tin about 25 x 20 cm/10 x 8 in.

2 Place the flour in a mixing bowl. Cut the butter into pieces and add to the bowl. Rub in with your fingertips until the mixture resembles fine breadcrumbs. Stir in the sugar and cinnamon. Add the egg yolk and enough milk to bring the mixture together to form a soft dough.

3 Roll out into a rectangle that almost fits the tin. Place in the tin and press out to fit with your fingers to fill the tin completely, pressing together any cracks in the dough.

4 Brush the top of the dough with beaten egg white and sprinkle the flaked almonds over the top. Sprinkle with sugar crystals or granulated sugar and bake for about 20 minutes until golden. Cut into pieces whilst still warm and transfer to a wire rack to cool completely.

Makes about 30
Prep time: 30 mins
Cook time: 20 mins

150 g/5 oz butter, softened
50 g/2 oz caster sugar

225 g/8 oz plain flour
100 g/4 oz chopped almonds, finely chopped
40 g/1½ oz granulated sugar
2 egg yolks, lightly beaten

Finnish shortbread

1 Preheat the oven to 180°C/350°F/Gas 4.

2 Beat the butter and caster sugar together until pale and fluffy. Beat in the flour and mix to a soft dough.

3 Divide the dough into 2 or 3 pieces and roll into long sausages about 1 cm/½ in thick. Cut into 5 cm/2 in lengths. Combine the nuts and granulated sugar. Dip each piece of dough into the egg yolks, then roll in the chopped nut mixture to coat. Place on baking sheets.

4 Bake for 20 minutes until golden. Cool on the baking sheets for a couple of minutes before transferring to a wire rack to cool completely.

TIP
You could use other nuts, such as chopped pecans, walnuts or hazelnuts instead of the almonds, if preferred.

Makes about 18
Prep time: 45 mins
Cook time: 5 mins

50 g/2 oz butter
50 g/2 oz caster sugar
1 egg, lightly beaten
4 tbsp double cream
50 g/2 oz self-raising flour

Tuiles

1 Preheat the oven to 220°C/425°F/Gas 7. Lightly grease
2 baking sheets.

2 Beat the butter and sugar together until pale and fluffy.
Gradually beat in the egg and cream. Carefully fold in the
flour.

3 Place about 6 dessertspoonfuls of the batter on the
baking sheet and spread each into a 7.5 cm/3 in circle. Bake
for 5 minutes until just golden around the edges.

4 Working quickly, remove the cookies from the baking sheet
with a palette knife and drape over a rolling pin to make a
curved shape. Allow to cool.

5 Repeat with the remaining batter until all the tuiles are
made, alternating the baking sheets, so that they have time to
cool between each batch.

VARIATION
Add some finely chopped pistachio nuts or flaked almonds
to the mixture.

Sponge
cakes

Serves 8
Prep time: 25 mins
Cook time: 25–30 mins

225 g/8 oz unsalted butter, softened
225 g/8 oz caster sugar
4 large eggs
225 g/8 oz plain flour
2 tsp baking powder

FILLING
115 g/4 oz mascarpone cheese
100 ml/3½ fl oz double cream
6 tbsp seedless raspberry jam
115 g/4 oz raspberries
icing sugar, to dust

Victoria sandwich

1 Grease and line two 20 cm/8 in sandwich tins, 4 cm/1½ in deep. Preheat the oven to 180°C/350°F/Gas 4.

2 Beat the butter and sugar together until creamy. Beat in the eggs one at a time, adding a tablespoon of the flour with each egg. Sieve in the rest of the flour and baking powder and fold in until evenly combined.

3 Divide the mixture between the cake tins, level and bake for 25–30 minutes or until springy to the touch. Cool in the tins for 5 minutes before turning out onto a wire rack to cool completely. Peel off the paper.

4 For the filling, stir together the mascarpone and cream until smooth and thick enough to spread. Spoon 4 tablespoons of the jam onto one cake and spread in an even layer, followed by the mascarpone cream. Lift the second cake layer on top. Chill until ready to serve.

5 Just before serving, warm the remaining jam and brush it over the top. Cover with raspberries and dust with icing sugar.

Serves 6
Prep time: 30 mins
Cook time: 30–35 mins

175 g/6 oz unsalted butter, softened
175 g/6 oz caster sugar, plus extra
for rolling out marzipan
3 large eggs
175 g/6 oz plain flour

2 tsp baking powder
75 g/3 oz ground rice
grated zest of 1 orange
few drops of orange food colouring
2 tbsp cocoa powder
2 tbsp milk
4 tbsp apricot jam
350 g/12 oz yellow marzipan

Choc-orange battenberg

1 Grease and line a 20 cm/8 in square cake tin and place a folded strip of greased foil down the centre of the tin to divide it in two. Preheat the oven to 180°C/350°F/Gas 4.

2 Beat the butter and sugar together until creamy. Beat in the eggs one at a time, adding a tablespoon of flour with each egg. Sieve in the rest of the flour and baking powder. Fold in with the ground rice. Spoon half the mix into another bowl.

3 Stir the orange zest and a little food colouring into one bowl and the cocoa powder and milk into the other. Spoon the orange mixture into one side of the tin and the cocoa mixture into the other, spreading the tops of both level.

4 Bake for 30–35 minutes until well risen and springy to the touch. Cool in the tin for 5 minutes before turning out onto a wire rack to cool completely. Remove the paper and foil.

5 Cut each cake in half lengthways to give 4 strips. Warm the jam, brush over the sides and layer two on top of the other two, alternating the colours. Brush the outside with jam. Roll out the marzipan thinly on a surface dusted with caster sugar and wrap around the cake. Press it in place and trim the edges.

Serves 8
Prep time: 20 mins
Cook time: 45 mins

150 g/5 oz unsalted butter, softened
175 g/6 oz golden caster sugar
2 large eggs
175 g/6 oz plain flour

2 tsp baking powder
1 tsp ground cinnamon
115 g/4 oz ground almonds
90 g/3½ oz sultanas
75 ml/3 fl oz milk
1–2 dessert apples, such as Granny Smith or Cox
juice of ½ lemon

Danish apple and sultana cake

1 Grease and line a 23 cm/9 in spring-clip tin. Preheat the oven to 190°C/375°F/Gas 5.

2 Beat the butter and 150 g/5 oz of the sugar together until smooth and creamy. Beat in the eggs one at a time, adding a tablespoon of the flour with each egg. Sieve in the rest of the flour, the baking powder and cinnamon. Add the almonds and sultanas and fold everything together until evenly combined. Finally stir in the milk.

3 Spoon the mixture into the tin and spread level. Peel, core and thinly slice the apples. Toss in a bowl with the lemon juice, then scatter over the top of the cake.

4 Dust with the remaining sugar and bake for 45 minutes or until just firm. Cool in the tin for 10 minutes before transferring the cake to a wire rack to cool completely and removing the paper.

Serves 8
Prep time: 30 mins
Cook time: 25 mins

175 g/6 oz unsalted butter,
softened
175 g/6 oz light muscovado sugar
1 tbsp coffee essence
3 large eggs
225 g/8 oz plain flour

2 tsp baking powder
1 tbsp milk
50 g/2 oz chopped walnuts

TO DECORATE
1 quantity of coffee buttercream,
see page 252
walnut halves and chopped walnuts
chocolate coffee beans

Walnut and coffee sponge

1 Grease and line two 20 cm/8 in sandwich tins, 4 cm/1^{1}/$_{2}$ in deep. Preheat the oven to 190°C/375°F/Gas 5.

2 In a mixing bowl, beat the butter with the sugar until creamy. Stir in the coffee essence, then beat in the eggs one at a time, adding a tablespoon of the flour with each egg. Sieve in the rest of the flour and baking powder and fold in. Finally stir in the milk and walnuts.

3 Divide the mixture between the tins and spread level. Bake for 25 minutes or until springy to the touch. Cool in the tins for 5 minutes, then turn out onto a wire rack to cool completely and remove papers.

4 To decorate, sandwich the cake layers with some of the buttercream and spread the rest over the top and sides. Top with walnut halves, a few chopped walnuts and chocolate coffee beans.

Serves 16
Prep time: 20 mins
Cook time: 25–30 mins

125 g/4¹/₂ oz plain flour
375 g/13 oz caster sugar
10 large egg whites

¹/₂ tsp cream of tartar
finely grated zest of 1 lemon
¹/₂ tsp vanilla extract

TO SERVE
icing sugar, to dust
a selection of fresh berries

Angel cake with fresh berries

1 Preheat the oven to 190°C/375°F/Gas 5.

2 Sieve the flour into a bowl and stir in half the sugar. In another large bowl, whisk the egg whites with the cream of tartar until standing in soft peaks. Whisk in the remaining sugar, a little at a time, until the egg whites are stiff.

3 Fold in the lemon zest, vanilla extract and flour mixture using a large metal spoon.

4 Spoon into an ungreased 23 cm/9 in angel cake tin, 10 cm/4 in deep, level and bake for 25–30 minutes or until a skewer pushed into the cake comes out clean.

5 Invert onto a wire rack and leave the cake to cool in the tin before running a knife around the edge to release it. Serve dusted with icing sugar and with a selection of fresh berries.

TIP
The tin should not be greased as this will prevent the cake from rising.

Serves 8
Prep time: 20 mins
Cook time: 12–15 mins

4 large eggs
115 g/4 oz caster sugar, plus extra
to dust
115 g/4 oz plain flour
1 tbsp warm water

FILLING
150 ml/5 fl oz double cream
2 tbsp lemon curd
175 g/6 oz strawberries, hulled and
roughly chopped

Swiss roll with strawberries

1 Grease and line a 33 x 23 cm/13 x 9 in Swiss roll tin.
Preheat the oven to 190°C/375°F/Gas 5.

2 Stand a large mixing bowl over a pan of simmering water,
making sure the bottom doesn't touch the water. Add the eggs
and sugar and whisk until pale and the mixture leaves a thick
trail when the beaters are lifted. Remove the bowl to the work
surface and continue whisking until the base of it feels cool.

3 Fold in the warm water with a large metal spoon, sieve the
flour over the top and gently fold in. Turn the mixture into
the tin, spreading it into the corners and bake for 12–15
minutes or until golden brown and just firm to the touch.

4 Sprinkle a sheet of baking parchment with caster sugar and
turn the cake out onto it. Remove the lining paper. Trim the
edges, then score the cake across 2.5 cm/1 in from one short
side without cutting all the way through. Roll up with the
parchment inside. Lift onto a wire rack and leave to cool.

5 For the filling, whisk the cream and lemon curd together
until thick. When ready to serve, unroll the cake, spread with
the lemon cream and scatter over the strawberries. Re-roll
without the parchment and dust with extra caster sugar.

Serves 8
Prep time: 30 mins
Cook time: 30 mins

175 g/6 oz unsalted butter, softened
115 g/4 oz caster sugar
2 tbsp clear honey
3 large eggs
225 g/ 8 oz plain flour

115 g/4 oz blueberries
2 tsp baking powder
$^1/_2$ tsp ground cinnamon

TO DECORATE
1 quantity of glacé icing,
see page 252

a selection of fresh berries and
currants

Iced honey sponge with fruits of the forest

1 Grease a 1.4 l/2$^1/_2$ pt ring tin and dust with flour. Preheat the oven to 180°C/350°F/Gas 4.

2 In a mixing bowl, beat the butter and sugar until creamy, then stir in the honey. Beat in the eggs one at a time, adding a tablespoon of flour with each egg. Dust the blueberries with a little of the remaining flour and sieve the rest with the baking powder and cinnamon into the bowl, then fold in together with the blueberries.

3 Spoon the mixture into the tin, level and bake for 30 minutes or until a skewer pushed into the cake comes out clean. Cool in the tin for 10 minutes before turning out onto a wire rack to cool completely.

4 To decorate, spread the glacé icing over the top of the cake, letting it run down the sides. Decorate with fresh berries and currants before the icing sets.

Serves 8
Prep time: 1 hour
Cook time: 40 mins

225 g/8 oz plain flour
1 tbsp baking powder
2 tbsp cocoa powder
200 g/7 oz light muscovado sugar
150 g/5 oz unsalted butter, melted
and cooled

3 large eggs
200 g/7 oz cooked pumpkin flesh,
mashed and cooled

TO DECORATE
1 quantity of orange buttercream,
see page 252
400 g/14 oz orange coloured
sugarpaste icing or marzipan and
small amounts of green, white and
black

Chocolate pumpkin cake

1 Grease and base line two 1.2 1/2 pt heatproof basins.
Preheat the oven to 180°C/350°F/Gas 4.

2 Sieve the flour, baking powder and cocoa powder into a
mixing bowl and stir in the sugar. In another bowl, beat
together the melted butter and eggs, then pour into the dry
ingredients, stirring until combined. Stir in the mashed
pumpkin.

3 Divide the mixture between the basins and spread level.
Bake for 40 minutes until a skewer pressed into the centre of
each cake comes out clean. Cool in the basins for 10 minutes
before turning out onto a wire rack to cool completely and
peeling off the papers.

4 To decorate, sandwich the two sponges together with some
of the buttercream and spread the rest over the outside. Roll
out the orange sugarpaste icing or marzipan and lift over the
cake, pressing it into place and marking 'pumpkin' ridges
down the sides with the handle of a wooden spoon. Cut
features from black and white icing or marzipan and a stalk
from green and fix in place with a dab of buttercream.

Serves 8–10
Prep time: 1 hour
Cook time: 25–30 mins

CHOCOLATE CAKE
175 g/6 oz unsalted butter, softened
175 g/6 oz light muscovado sugar
3 large eggs
175 g/6 oz plain flour

1¹/₂ tbsp cocoa powder
1¹/₂ tsp baking powder

TO DECORATE
1 quantity of milk chocolate
ganache, see page 253
white and coloured sugarpaste icing
or marzipan
small sweets

Toy town train sponge

1 To make the cake, grease and base line two 20 cm/8 in sandwich tins, 4 cm/1¹/₂ in deep. Preheat the oven to 180°C/350°F/Gas 4.

2 Beat the butter and sugar together until creamy. Beat in the eggs one at a time, adding a tablespoon of the flour with each egg. Sieve in the rest of the flour, the cocoa powder and baking powder, then fold in.

3 Divide the mixture between the tins and spread level. Bake for 25–30 minutes or until springy to the touch. Cool in the tins for 5 minutes before turning out onto a wire rack to cool completely. Remove the papers.

4 Sandwich the cake layers with some of the ganache and spread the remainder over the top and sides.

5 Cut out shapes from thinly rolled, coloured sugarpaste icing or marzipan for a train engine, wheels and carriages and press in place while the icing is still wet. Top the carriages with sweets for cargo and add clouds of steam cut from white sugarpaste from the engine funnel.

Serves 8–10
Prep time: 45 mins plus setting
Cook time: 40–45 mins

150 g/5 oz dark chocolate, chopped
2 tbsp strong black coffee
115 g/4 oz unsalted butter, softened
115 g/4 oz light muscovado sugar
3 large eggs, separated
65 g/2¹/₂ oz plain flour
1 tsp baking powder
65 g/2¹/₂ oz potato flour

FILLING AND DECORATION
225 g/8 oz full-fat cream cheese
75 g/3 oz caster sugar
200 g/7 oz white chocolate, chopped
250 ml/9 fl oz double cream
1 tbsp cold strong black coffee
chocolate hearts
cocoa powder, to dust

Mocha chocolate heart

1 Grease and line a heart-shaped tin measuring 20 cm/8 in across its widest part. Preheat the oven to 180°C/350°F/Gas 4.

2 Melt the chocolate with the coffee in a bowl over a pan of simmering water. In another bowl, beat the butter and sugar together until creamy. Beat in the egg yolks and stir in the melted, cooled chocolate.

3 Sieve in the plain flour, baking powder and potato flour, then fold in. Whisk the egg whites until stiff, stir in 1 tablespoon, then fold in the remainder. Spoon into the tin, level and bake for 40–45 minutes or until a skewer pushed into the centre comes out clean. Cool in the tin for 10 minutes, then turn out onto a wire rack to cool. Remove the paper.

4 Whisk the cream cheese and sugar together until smooth. Melt the chocolate, stirring until smooth and add to the cream cheese. Whip, then fold in 150 ml/5 fl oz of the cream. Split the cake in half, then sandwich together with the filling. Chill until firm. Whip the remaining cream and coffee and spread over the top. Decorate with the hearts and dust with cocoa powder.

Serves: about 60
Prep time: 2–2$1/2$ hours plus setting

Cook time: 40–45 mins
(15 cm/6 in cake),
1–1$1/4$ hours (23 cm/9 in) cake),
1$1/2$ hours (30 cm/12 in) cake)

Wedding bells

CAKES

Top tier -15cm/6in:
115 g/4 oz unsalted butter, softened
115 g/4 oz caster sugar
2 large eggs
175 g/6 oz plain flour
1 tsp vanilla essence
1$1/2$ tsp baking powder
1 tbsp milk

Middle tier - 23cm/9in:
225 g/8 oz unsalted butter, softened
225 g/8 oz caster sugar
4 large eggs
350 g/12 oz plain flour
1$1/2$ tsp vanilla essence
1 tbsp baking powder
2$1/2$ tbsp milk

Bottom tier - 30cm/12in:
450 g/1 lb unsalted butter, softened
450 g/1 lb caster sugar
8 large eggs
700 g/1$1/2$ lb plain flour
2$1/2$ tsp vanilla essence
2 tbsp baking powder
5 tbsp milk

TO DECORATE

Top tier: 1 quantity of white
chocolate icing, see page 252

Middle tier: 1$1/2$ quantities of white
chocolate icing

Bottom tier: 2$1/2$ quantities of white
chocolate icing

fresh flowers

butterflies made from edible wafer
paper and piped writing icing

1 Grease and line one 15 cm/6 in, one 23 cm/9 in and one
30 cm/12 in deep, round cake tin. Preheat the oven to
180°C/350°F/Gas 4.

2 For each tier, beat the butter and sugar together until
creamy. Beat in the eggs one at a time, adding one
tablespoon of the flour with each egg. Stir in the vanilla
extract. Sieve in the rest of the flour and baking powder and

continued next page

sponge cakes   91

fold in. Finally stir in the milk. Spoon into the tins, level and bake the top tier for 40–45 minutes, the middle for 1–1¼ hours and the bottom for 1½ hours or until a skewer pushed into the centre comes out clean. Cool in the tins for 10 minutes before turning out onto wire racks to cool completely and peeling off the lining papers.

3 To decorate, stand each tier on a wire rack over a plate or baking sheet and pour over the icing, smoothing it over the top and sides with a palette knife. Leave in a cool place until set.

4 To assemble, place the bottom tier on a board or large platter and stack the middle and top tiers on top. Decorate with fresh flowers and edible wafer paper butterflies.

TIPS

To make the butterflies, trace shapes onto edible wafer paper. Cut them out with scissors and fold carefully in half. Open out so they are 'V' shaped, decorate with piped coloured writing icing and leave to set on crumpled cling film.

If transporting the cake, keep the tiers separate and assemble on arrival.

The cakes can be stacked directly on top of each other or the two upper tiers placed on thin cake cards, which will make them easier to separate and cut.

Serves 10–12
Prep time: 30 mins plus soaking
Cook time: 50 mins

275 g/10 oz plain flour
2 1/2 tsp baking powder
175 ml/6 fl oz sunflower oil
175 g/6 oz golden caster sugar
5 large eggs

grated zest of 2 large or 3 small lemons
175 g/6 oz natural Greek yoghurt

SYRUP
115 g/4 oz golden caster sugar
50 ml/2 fl oz water
1/2 tsp ground cinnamon
grated zest and juice of 1 small orange

Greek Easter cake

1 Grease and flour a 2.4 1/4 pt bundt tin or a round cake tin with a similar capacity. Preheat the oven to 170°C/325°F/Gas 3.

2 Sieve the flour and baking powder into a bowl. Measure the sunflower oil into a jug, then add the sugar, eggs, lemon zest and yoghurt and whisk until mixed. Pour into the dry ingredients and stir until evenly combined.

3 Spoon into the tin and bake for 50 minutes or until a skewer pushed into the cake comes out clean.

4 When the cake is almost cooked, make the syrup. Put the sugar, water and cinnamon into a small pan and heat gently until the sugar dissolves. Bring to the boil and leave to bubble for 2 minutes. Remove from the heat and stir in the orange zest and juice.

5 When the cake is ready, remove from the oven and leave to cool in the tin for 5 minutes. Turn it out onto a cooling rack set over a plate and spoon over half the syrup. Leave for 10 minutes to soak in, then spoon over the rest and leave the cake to cool completely.

Serves 8
Prep time: 45 mins
Cook time: 50 mins

150 g/5 oz unsalted butter
150 g/5 oz caster sugar
1 tsp vanilla essence
4 large eggs, separated
75 g/3 oz plain flour
1 tsp baking powder
115 g/4 oz ground almonds

FROSTING AND DECORATION
1 tbsp maple syrup
50 g/2 oz unsalted butter, cut into small pieces
1 tbsp milk
$1/2$ tsp vanilla essence
225 g/8 oz icing sugar
stars cut from white sugarpaste icing, made 1 day ahead and left until hard
edible silver paint and edible glitter
ribbon

Starry starry night cake

1 Grease and line a 20 cm/8 in round cake tin. Preheat the oven to 180°C/350°F/Gas 4.

2 Beat the butter and caster sugar together until creamy, then stir in the vanilla and egg yolks. In a separate bowl, whisk the egg whites until standing in soft peaks. Sieve the flour and baking powder into the creamed mixture, then stir in with the almonds. Stir in a spoonful of the whisked egg whites to soften the mixture, then fold in the rest with a large metal spoon.

3 Spoon the mixture into the tin, level and bake for 50 minutes or until a skewer pushed into the centre comes out clean. Cool in the tin for 10 minutes before removing to a wire rack to cool completely and peeling off the paper.

4 For the frosting, melt the maple syrup, butter and milk in a small pan. Stir in the vanilla. Sieve the icing sugar into a bowl, then pour over the syrup mixture, stirring until smooth. Cool, then beat with a wooden spoon until thick enough to spread over the top and sides of the cake. Add stars outlined with silver paint. Dust with glitter and tie a ribbon around the cake.

Serves 10–12
Prep time: 40 mins
Cook time: 1 hour

200 g/7 oz dark chocolate, chopped
200 g/7 oz unsalted butter, cut in
small pieces
115 ml/4 fl oz cold black coffee
175 g/6 oz plain flour
1 tsp baking powder
1/2 tsp bicarbonate of soda

115 g/4 oz light muscovado sugar
115 g/4 oz caster sugar
3 large eggs
75 ml/3 fl oz buttermilk

TO DECORATE
1 quantity of marshmallow frosting,
see page 252

sugarpaste or marzipan flowers
and leaves

sugar sprinkles

Chocolate buttermilk cake

1 Grease a 1.8 l/3 pt ring tin or a round cake tin with a similar capacity. Preheat the oven to 160°C/325°F/Gas 3.

2 Put the chocolate and butter in a pan, add the coffee and heat gently until melted. Stir until smooth.

3 Sieve the flour, baking powder and bicarbonate of soda into a bowl and stir in the sugars. In another bowl, beat the eggs with the buttermilk, then pour onto the dry ingredients with the melted chocolate mixture.

4 Stir until everything is just combined, pour into the tin and bake for about 1 hour or until a skewer pushed into the cake comes out clean.

5 Leave to cool in the tin before turning out. When cold, split in half horizontally and sandwich with some of the frosting.

6 Spread more frosting over the top and sides. Decorate with sugarpaste or marzipan flowers and leaves and sugar sprinkles.

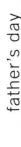

Serves 10
Prep time: 45 mins
Cook time: 45 mins

225 g/8 oz unsalted butter, softened
225 g/8 oz caster sugar
4 large eggs
225 g/8 oz plain flour
1 tsp vanilla essence

2 tsp baking powder
green food colouring

TO DECORATE
1 quantity of orange buttercream,
see page 252

coloured sugarpaste icing or
marzipan

Rainbow madeira with orange buttercream

1 Grease and line a 20 cm/8 in square cake tin. Preheat the oven to 180°C/350°F/Gas 4.

2 In a mixing bowl, beat the butter and sugar together until creamy. Beat in the eggs one at a time, adding a tablespoon of the flour with each egg. Stir in the vanilla, sieve in the rest of the flour and baking powder and fold in until evenly combined. Spoon half the mixture into a separate bowl and tint with a few drops of green food colouring.

3 Spoon alternate tablespoons of the mixture into the tin and bake for 45 minutes or until a skewer pushed into the centre comes out clean. Cool in the tin for 10 minutes before turning out onto a wire rack to cool completely and peeling off the paper.

4 Spread the buttercream over the cake and decorate with Dad's favourite tie, hat, socks and scarf. To make these, roll out the coloured icing or marzipan thinly on a board dusted with icing sugar. Cut out shapes in various colours with a sharp knife, dampen with a litte water and press together.

Serves 12
Prep time: 20 mins
Cook time: 55 mins–1 hour

250 g/9 oz unsalted butter, softened
250 g/9 oz caster sugar
4 large eggs
375 g/13 oz plain flour

175 g/6 oz raspberries, lightly crushed
1 tbsp baking powder
100 g/3½ oz white chocolate, chopped
3 tbsp milk
icing sugar, to dust

Raspberry sponge ring

1 Grease and flour a 2.4 1/4 pt bundt tin or use a square or round cake tin with a similar capacity. Preheat the oven to 180°C/350°F/Gas 4.

2 In a mixing bowl, beat the butter and sugar together until creamy. Beat in the eggs one at a time, adding a tablespoon of the flour with each egg. Dust the raspberries with a little of the remaining flour. Sieve the rest of the flour into the bowl with the baking powder. Fold in with the white chocolate and raspberries. Finally stir in the milk.

3 Spoon the mixture into the tin, level and bake for 55 minutes to 1 hour or until a skewer pushed into the cake comes out clean. Cool in the tin for 10 minutes before turning out onto a wire rack to cool completely.

4 Serve the cake dusted with icing sugar.

TIP
Dusting the raspberries with a little flour before adding them to the cake mix prevents them from sinking during baking.

Serves 8
Prep time: 45 mins plus setting
Cook time: 20 mins

150 g/5 oz dark chocolate, chopped
5 large eggs, separated
150 g/5 oz caster sugar
2 tbsp cocoa powder

FILLING AND DECORATION
150 g/5 oz unsweetened chestnut purée
40 g/1½ oz icing sugar, plus extra to dust
150 ml/5 fl oz double cream
¾ quantity of dark chocolate icing, see page 252
edible gold leaf (optional)

Bûche de Noël

1 Grease and line a 33 x 23 cm/13 x 9 in Swiss roll tin. Preheat the oven to 180°C/350°F/Gas 4.

2 Melt the chocolate in a bowl over a pan of simmering water, stirring until smooth. In a large mixing bowl, whisk the egg yolks and sugar together until thick, creamy and pale-coloured. Sieve in the cocoa and fold in with the cooled, melted chocolate. In another bowl, whisk the egg whites until stiff. Stir 1 tablespoon into the chocolate mixture before gently folding in the rest.

3 Pour the mixture into the tin, spreading it to the corners, and bake for 20 minutes or until just firm to the touch.

4 Turn out onto a sheet of baking parchment and peel off the lining paper. Cover with a clean tea towel and leave to cool.

5 To fill and decorate, beat the chestnut purée and icing sugar together until smooth, then slowly whisk in the cream until light and fluffy. Spread over the roulade to within 1 cm/½ in of the edges and roll up from one long side. Pour the chocolate icing over, spreading with a palette knife to cover evenly and leave to set. Dust with icing sugar and, if wished, add small pieces of edible gold leaf.

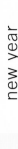

Serves 10–12
Prep time: 30 mins
Cook time: 30 mins

250 g/9 oz plain flour
2 tsp baking powder
1 tsp ground cinnamon
200 g/7 oz light muscovado sugar
2 large eggs
200 ml/7 fl oz sunflower oil
2 small bananas, unpeeled weight
about 225 g/8 oz

150 g/5 oz grated carrot
50 g/2 oz sultanas
50 g/2 oz chopped walnuts

TO DECORATE
1 quantity of cream cheese frosting
with ½ tsp ground cinnamon added,
see page 253
coloured sugarpaste icing or
marzipan

Carrot and banana cake

1 Grease and line two 20 cm/8 in sandwich tins, 4 cm/1½ in
deep. Preheat the oven to 180°C/350°F/Gas 4.

2 Sieve the flour, baking powder and cinnamon into a bowl
and stir in the sugar. Liquidize the eggs, oil and bananas
together until smooth and creamy, then fold into the dry
ingredients. Finally fold in the carrot, sultanas and walnuts.

3 Divide the mixture between the tins, level, and bake for
30 minutes or until a skewer inserted into the centre of each
cake comes out clean. Cool in the tins for 30 minutes before
turning out onto a wire rack to cool completely and peeling
off the papers.

4 To decorate, sandwich the cake layers with some of the
frosting and spread the rest on top.
Arrange carrots and bananas modelled
from sugarpaste or marzipan around
the edge.

TIP
The riper the
bananas, the
sweeter and more
fragrant the finished
cake will be.

Serves 9
Prep time: 30 mins
Cook time: 45 mins

200 g/7 oz plain flour
2 tsp baking powder
150 g/5 oz unsalted butter, cut into small pieces
200 g/7oz light muscovado sugar
grated zest of 3 limes
2 large eggs

300 ml/10 fl oz buttermilk

TOPPING
25 g/1 oz unsalted butter, cut into small pieces
50 g/2 oz plain flour
5 tbsp light muscovado sugar
75 g/3 oz unsalted cashews, roughly chopped
juice of 3 limes

Lime drizzle cake with crunchy cashews

1 Grease and line a 19 cm/7 in square cake tin. Preheat the oven to 180°C/350°F/Gas 4.

2 Sieve the flour and baking powder into a mixing bowl, rub in the butter, then stir in the sugar. In another bowl, beat together the lime zest, eggs and buttermilk, pour into the flour mixture and whisk until evenly combined. Pour into the tin.

3 For the topping, rub the butter into the flour and stir in 1 tablespoon of the sugar and all of the cashews. Scatter over the top of the cake mixture.

4 Bake for 45 minutes or until a skewer pushed into the centre comes out clean. Stir together the rest of the sugar and the lime juice and spoon over the cake as soon as it comes out of the oven.

5 Leave to cool in the tin for 30 minutes before turning out onto a wire rack and removing the paper. Cut into squares and eat warm or cold.

Serves 8
Prep time: 30 mins
Cook time: 15–18 mins

4 large eggs, separated
150 g/5 oz caster sugar
3 tbsp plain flour
115 g/4 oz toasted hazelnuts, finely ground

FILLING
150 ml/5 fl oz double cream
2 tbsp apricot brandy or juice from the apricot can
caster sugar, to dust
411 g/14^1/$_2$ oz can of apricot halves in fruit juice, drained and chopped

Hazelnut and apricot roll

1 Grease and line a 33 x 23 cm/13 x 9 in Swiss roll tin. Preheat the oven to 180°C/350°F/Gas 4.

2 In a bowl, whisk the egg yolks and 125 g/4^1/$_2$ oz of the sugar until thick and pale-coloured. Sieve over the flour, scatter over the hazelnuts and fold in with a large metal spoon.

3 In another bowl, whisk the egg whites until stiff and gradually whisk in the remaining sugar until glossy. Stir a large spoonful into the egg yolk mixture, before carefully folding in the rest. Pour into the tin, level and bake for 15–18 minutes or until risen and just firm to the touch. Remove from the oven, cover with a damp tea cloth and leave to cool.

4 For the filling, whip the cream with the apricot brandy or juice until holding its shape. Sprinkle a sheet of baking parchment with caster sugar, turn out the sponge onto it and remove the lining paper. Spread the cream over the sponge to within 1 cm/^{1}/$_2$ in of the edges and add the chopped apricots.

5 Roll up the sponge starting from one short side. Transfer to a serving plate and chill until ready to serve. Sprinkle with extra sugar just before serving.

Serves 8–10
Prep time: 30 mins
Cook time: 45 mins

75 g/3 oz finely chopped fresh or tinned mango flesh
225 g/8 oz plain flour
175 g/6 oz unsalted butter, softened
200 g/7 oz golden caster sugar
3 large eggs

1 tbsp baking powder
1 tbsp finely chopped or grated, chilled, creamed coconut
2 tbsp milk

ICING AND DECORATION
3 passion fruit
150 g/5 oz icing sugar
fresh coconut shavings

Coconut and mango cake

1 Grease and flour a 1.6 l/2¾ pt kugelhopf tin or another tin with a similar capacity. Preheat the oven to 180°C/350°F/Gas 4.

2 Dust the chopped mango with a little of the flour. Put the butter, caster sugar, eggs, remaining flour and baking powder in a mixing bowl and add the grated coconut and milk. Whisk until the mixture is smooth and creamy. Finally stir in the mango.

3 Spoon into the tin, level and bake for 45 minutes or until a skewer pushed into the centre comes out clean. Cool in the tin for 5 minutes before turning out onto a wire rack to cool completely.

4 To make the icing, halve the passion fruit, scoop out the pulp and seeds of one fruit and add to the icing sugar. Scoop out the pulp and seeds from the other two into a small bowl and heat gently until the seeds separate from the pulp. Push through a sieve and stir the juice into the icing sugar until evenly mixed in.

5 Spread the icing over the top of the cake letting it run down the sides. Decorate with shavings of fresh coconut.

Serves 10
Prep time: 20 mins
Cook time: 50 mins

115 g/4 oz honey
150 g/5 oz dark muscovado sugar
1 tsp ground anise seed
1 tsp ground ginger

1 tsp ground cinnamon
1 tsp finely grated orange or lemon zest
100 ml/3½ fl oz water
250 g/9 oz plain flour
2 tsp baking powder
1 large egg, beaten
75 g/3 oz chopped pecans

Pecan pain d'épice

1 Grease and line a 1.2 1/2 pt loaf tin. Preheat the oven to 170°C/325°F/Gas 3.

2 Put the honey, sugar, ground spices, orange or lemon zest and water in a pan and heat gently until the honey and sugar melt, stirring regularly with a wooden spoon.

3 Sieve the flour and baking powder together and add to the melted mixture with the egg and pecans. Stir until evenly combined.

4 Spoon the mixture into the tin and bake for 50 minutes or until a skewer pushed into the centre comes out clean. Leave to cool in the tin for 30 minutes before turning out onto a wire rack and removing the paper. Eat warm or cold. The cake has quite a dry texture, so is also good spread with butter.

TIP
Ground anise seed
can be found in
Middle Eastern
stores but you could
substitute 1 tsp
fenugreek or
caraway seeds.

Serves 8–10
Prep time: 20 mins
Cook time: 45 mins

4 sprigs of soft fresh rosemary, each about 7.5 cm/3 in long
175 g/6 oz unsalted butter, softened

175 g/6 oz caster sugar
finely grated zest of 1 small orange
3 large eggs
225 g/8 oz plain flour
2 tsp baking powder
icing sugar, to dust

Orange and rosemary madeira cake

1 Grease and flour a 1.5 l/2½ pt bundt tin. Preheat the oven to 180°C/350°F/Gas 4.

2 Strip the rosemary leaves from their stalks and chop very finely. In a mixing bowl, beat the butter until creamy, then gradually beat in the sugar, orange zest and rosemary.

3 Beat in the eggs one at a time, adding a tablespoon of the flour with each egg. Sieve in the rest of the flour and baking powder and fold in.

4 Spoon the mixture into the tin, level and bake for 45 minutes or until a skewer pushed into the centre comes out clean. Leave to cool in the tin for 10 minutes before turning out onto a wire rack to cool completely.

5 Serve dusted with icing sugar.

TIP
Be sure to use rosemary leaves that are young, green and tender as older ones will be tough and dry.

Serves 8
Prep time: 30 mins
Cook time: 45 mins

150 g/5 oz unsalted butter, softened
200 g/7 oz caster sugar
finely grated zest of 1 orange and
2 lemons
4 large eggs
150 g/5 oz plain flour
2 tsp baking powder
115 g/4 oz ground almonds

SPICED SYRUP AND DECORATION
juice of 1 orange and 2 lemons
65 g/2¹/₂ oz caster sugar
1 tsp ground cinnamon
¹/₂ tsp ground mixed spice
1 orange, peeled and sliced
2 tbsp chopped pistachios
2 tbsp orange jelly marmalade,
optional (see method)

Citrus syrup cake

1 Grease and line a 20 cm/8 in round cake tin. Preheat the
oven to 170°C/325°F/Gas 3.

2 Cream the butter and sugar together with the citrus zests.
Beat in the eggs one at a time, adding a tablespoon of the flour
with each egg. Sieve in the rest of the flour and baking powder
and fold in with the ground almonds.

3 Spoon into the tin, level and bake for 45 minutes or until a
skewer pushed into the centre comes out clean.

4 To make the syrup, put the citrus juices and sugar in a small
pan and add the spices. Heat gently until the sugar has
dissolved, then simmer for 2 minutes. Spoon over the cake as
soon as it comes out of the oven and leave to cool in the tin.

5 Turn the cake out, remove the paper and decorate with
orange segments and chopped pistachios. If not serving
immediately, brush the segments with the warmed jelly
marmalade to prevent them from drying out.

Serves 8
Prep time: 30 mins
Cook time: 30 mins

3 large eggs
150 g/5 oz golden caster sugar
90 g/3½ oz plain flour
1 tsp ground ginger

TO DECORATE
8 tbsp apricot jam
1 tbsp lemon juice
5 slices of pineapple, fresh or
tinned in fruit juice, chopped
50 g/2 oz raspberries

Ginger genoese with pineapple

1 Grease and line a 23 cm/9 in spring-clip or round cake tin. Preheat the oven to 180°C/350°F/Gas 4.

2 Put the eggs and sugar in a mixing bowl, stand the bowl over a pan of simmering water, without letting the bottom of the bowl touch the water, and whisk for about 5 minutes or until pale and mousse-like. Remove the bowl to the work surface and continue whisking until the base of it feels cool.

3 Sieve in the flour and ginger, then fold in gently with a large metal spoon. Pour into the tin, tap the tin lightly on the work surface to release any air bubbles and bake for 30 minutes or until the cake is just shrinking from the sides of the tin and springs back when pressed.

4 Cool in the tin for 10 minutes before turning out onto a wire rack to cool completely. Remove the paper.

5 To decorate, heat the jam with the lemon juice, then sieve to remove any large pieces of fruit. Brush the top of the cake with half the jam and arrange the chopped pineapple and raspberries on top. Brush with the rest of the jam.

Serves 9
Prep time: 30 mins
Cook time: 40–45 mins plus time for mashed potatoes

200 g/7 oz unsalted butter, softened
200 g/7 oz caster sugar
finely grated zest of 3 lemons
4 large eggs
175 g/6 oz rice flour

225 g/8 oz cooked potatoes, mashed and cooled
2 tsp gluten-free baking powder
2 tbsp poppy seeds

TO DECORATE
1 quantity of lemon glacé icing, see page 252
sugar sprinkles

Lemon and poppy seed rice cake

1 Grease and line a 19 cm/7 in square cake tin. Preheat the oven to 180°C/350°F/Gas 4.

2 Beat the butter, sugar and lemon zest together until creamy. Beat in the eggs one at a time, adding a tablespoon of the rice flour with each egg. Stir in the rest of the rice flour, the mashed potatoes, baking powder and poppy seeds.

3 Spoon into the tin, level and bake for 40–45 minutes or until a skewer pushed into the centre comes out clean. Cool in the tin for 10 minutes before turning out onto a wire rack to cool completely.

4 To decorate, drizzle or spread the icing over the cake and scatter with sugar sprinkles.

TIP
The same quantity of ground almonds or polenta could replace the rice flour.

gluten-free

Serves 8
Prep time: 20 mins
Cook time: 40 mins plus cooking time for sweet potatoes

175 g/6 oz unsalted butter, softened
175 g/6 oz caster sugar
4 large eggs
175 g/6 oz ground almonds

225 g/8 oz steamed sweet potatoes (about 2 medium), mashed and cooled
finely grated zest of 1 large orange
2 tsp gluten-free baking powder

DRIZZLE
6 tbsp icing sugar
1 tbsp orange juice
fine shreds of orange zest

Sweet potato and orange drizzle cake

1 Grease and line a 20 cm/8 in round cake tin. Preheat the oven to 180°C/350°F/Gas 4.

2 Beat the butter and sugar in a mixing bowl until creamy. Beat in the eggs one at a time, adding a tablespoon of the ground almonds with each egg. Stir in the remaining almonds, sweet potato mash, orange zest and baking powder.

3 Spoon into the tin, level and bake for 40 minutes or until a skewer inserted into the centre comes out clean.

4 Cool in the tin for 15 minutes before turning out onto a wire rack to cool completely and peeling off the paper.

5 Stir the orange juice into the icing sugar and drizzle over the cake. Decorate with the orange zest.

TIP
Gluten-free baking powder is available from larger supermarkets, check labels of containers before buying.

Serves 12
Prep time: 40 mins
Cook time: 30 mins

2 large eggs
150 ml/5 fl oz sunflower oil
175 g/6 oz apricots halves, fresh or tinned in juice, chopped
275 g/10 oz plain flour
1 tbsp baking powder
225 g/8 oz grated carrots

200 ml/7 fl oz unsweetened orange juice

FROSTING
50 g/2oz unsalted butter, softened
175 g/6 oz full-fat cream cheese
2 tsp unsweetened orange juice
extra apricot halves, fresh or tinned in juice, sliced
2 tbsp chopped pistachios
sugar-free sweetener (optional)

Apricot bars with cream cheese

1 Grease and line a 19 x 27.5 cm/7 x 11 in tin – a small roasting tin works well. Preheat the oven to 180°C/350°F/Gas 4.

2 Put the eggs in a mixing bowl and slowly whisk in the oil in a thin stream so it is incorporated smoothly into the eggs and the mixture is creamy and pale-coloured. Dust the apricots with a little of the flour.

3 Sieve the remaining flour and baking powder into the bowl and fold in with the carrots, apricots and orange juice.

4 Spoon into the tin and bake for 30 minutes or until a skewer pushed into the centre comes out clean. Cool in the tin for 10 minutes before turning out onto a wire rack to cool and peeling off the paper.

5 For the frosting, whisk together the butter, cream cheese and orange juice until smooth. Add a little sugar-free sweetener, if desired. Spread over the top of the cake and cut into 12 bars. Decorate each one with sliced apricots and chopped pistachios.

Serves 8
Prep time: 30 mins
Cook time: 50 mins

75 g/3 oz blueberries
115 g/4 oz plain flour
175 g/6 oz ground almonds
110 g/3½ oz caster sugar
3 large eggs, beaten
75 ml/3 fl oz sunflower oil

1½ tsp baking powder
5 tbsp coconut milk

ICING AND DECORATION
50 g/2 oz icing sugar
about 1 tbsp coconut milk
2 tbsp desiccated coconut,
lightly toasted
extra blueberries

Blueberry and coconut cake

1 Grease and line a 1.2 1/2 pt loaf tin. Preheat the oven to
180°C/350°F/Gas 4.

2 Dust the blueberries with a little of the flour. Put the
almonds, sugar, eggs, oil, baking powder, coconut milk and the
remaining flour in a large mixing bowl and whisk or beat
together until smooth. Stir in the blueberries.

3 Spoon the mixture into the tin and bake for 50 minutes or
until a skewer pushed into the centre comes out clean. Cool in
the tin for 10 minutes before turning out onto a wire rack to
cool completely. Remove the paper.

4 To decorate, stir the icing sugar and enough coconut milk
together to make a smooth, runny icing and drizzle over the
cake. Top with toasted desiccated coconut and extra blueberries.

TIP
Instead of blueberries, the
cake could be made with
redcurrants, blackcurrants
or lingonberries.

Chocolate

Makes 24
Prep time: 10 mins
Cook time: 25–30 mins

175 g/6 oz butter
175 g/6 oz caster sugar
3 eggs

175 g/6 oz self-raising flour
1 tsp baking powder
100 g/3½ oz ready-to-eat apricots, chopped
100 g/3½ oz good quality white chocolate, chopped
1 tbsp icing sugar, sieved

Apricot & white chocolate tray bake

1 Grease and line a 30 x 20 cm/12 x 8 in tray bake tin. Preheat the oven to 180°C/350°F/Gas 4.

2 In a mixing bowl, cream the butter and sugar together until light and fluffy. Beat in the eggs, flour and baking powder.

3 Mix in the apricots and white chocolate. Spread evenly into the tin and bake for 25–20 minutes or until firm to the touch and golden.

4 Cool in the tin for 5 minutes before turning out onto a wire rack to cool completely. Dust with icing sugar and cut into fingers.

TIP
Replace the apricots with dried apple and the white chocolate with dark chocolate.

Makes 8–10 slices
Prep time: 15 mins
Cook time: 50 mins–1 hour

225 g/8 oz butter
225 g/8 oz caster sugar

4 eggs, beaten
a few drops of vanilla extract
225 g/8 oz self-raising flour
1 tbsp cocoa powder
100 g/3¹/₂ oz plain chocolate

Chocolate marble slice

1 Grease and line a 900 g/2 lb loaf tin. Preheat the oven to 180°C/350°F/Gas 4.

2 In a mixing bowl, cream together the butter and sugar until light and fluffy, then gradually beat in the eggs and vanilla. Fold in the flour.

3 Transfer half the mixture to another bowl. Sift and fold the cocoa powder into this portion.

4 Break the chocolate into a small heatproof bowl and set over a pan of barely simmering water. Stir until the chocolate melts. Leave to cool slightly, then fold into the chocolate mixture.

5 Put alternative spoonfuls of the chocolate and plain mixtures into the loaf tin. Use a knife to swirl together creating a marbled effect.

6 Bake for 50 minutes–1 hour or until well risen and firm to the touch. Turn out onto a wire rack to cool. Serve sliced.

VARIATION
Add the finely grated zest of 1 lemon or 1 orange or chopped stem ginger to the plain sponge mix. For a spicy note add ¹/₂ tsp ground cinnamon to the chocolate sponge mix.

Makes 14 slices
Prep time: 30 mins
Cook time: 1–1¼ hours

200 g/7 oz dark chocolate (min. 70–75% cocoa solids)
200 g/7 oz butter, cubed
1 tbsp instant coffee granules
85 g/3 oz self-raising flour
85 g/3 oz plain flour
¼ tsp bicarbonate of soda
400 g/14 oz light soft brown sugar

3 tbsp cocoa powder
3 eggs, beaten
5 tbsp buttermilk or soured cream

GANACHE
200 g/7 oz dark chocolate (min. 70–75% cocoa solids), chopped
50 g/1¾ oz butter
284 ml/10 fl oz carton double cream
2 tbsp caster sugar
white and dark chocolate curls (see page 253), to decorate

The ultimate chocolate cake

1 Grease and line a 20 cm/7 in deep, round, loose-bottomed cake tin. Preheat the oven to 160°C/325°F/Gas 3.

2 Break the chocolate into a medium saucepan together with the butter and coffee. Add 125 ml/4 fl oz boiling water. Warm through over a low heat, stirring until melted and smooth.

3 Put all the dry ingredients into a large bowl. Make a well in the centre and add the eggs and milk or cream. Pour on the warm chocolate and mix to a smooth batter. Pour into the cake tin and bake for 1–1¼ hours or until a skewer inserted in the centre comes out clean. Leave to cool in the tin, then turn out onto a wire rack to cool completely. Cut into 3 horizontal layers.

4 To make the ganache, place the chocolate and butter in a mixing bowl. Heat the cream and sugar together in a saucepan and when just scalding, pour onto the chocolate. Cover and leave for a few minutes, then stir until smooth and glossy.

5 Sandwich the layers together with some of the ganache, then pour the rest over the cake. Decorate with chocolate curls.

Serves 8–10
Prep time: 25 mins
Cook time: 1¹/₄ hours

225 g/8 oz self-raising flour
40 g/1¹/₂ oz cocoa powder
1 level tbsp baking powder
¹/₂ tsp salt
2 large eggs
175 ml/6 fl oz semi-skimmed milk
75 g/2³/₄ oz caster sugar

100 g/3¹/₂ oz butter, melted
250 g/9 oz firm dessert plums,
stoned and finely chopped

TOPPING
25 g/1 oz butter
75 g/2³/₄ oz self-raising flour
75 g/2³/₄ oz demerara sugar
50 g/1³/₄ oz chopped toasted
hazelnuts
25 g/1 oz good quality white or milk
chocolate chips

Chocolate streusel cake

1 Grease and line a 20 cm/8 in spring-form cake tin. Preheat
the oven to 190°C/375°F/Gas 5.

2 Place the flour, cocoa powder, baking powder and salt into a
large bowl.

3 In another large bowl whisk together the eggs, milk and
sugar, then whisk in the melted butter.

4 Sift the dry ingredients onto the egg mixture and swiftly
fold in, together with the plums. Don't worry if the mixture
looks lumpy; it must not be over-stirred. Spoon into the tin.

5 For the topping, rub the butter into the flour to resemble
breadcrumbs, then stir in the sugar and hazelnuts with 1 tbsp
cold water to form a rough crumble. Scatter over the cake.

6 Bake for 1¹/₄ hours until risen and springy. (Cover the tin
with foil if the cake darkens too quickly). As soon as it is ready,
scatter on the chocolate chips. Leave to cool in the tin for 30
minutes before transferring to a wire rack to cool completely.

Serves 8
Prep time: 3–5 mins
Cook time: 25–35 mins

175 g/6 oz self-raising flour
25 g/1 oz cocoa powder
1 rounded tsp baking powder
125 g/4½ oz caster sugar
150 ml/5 fl oz groundnut oil

150 ml/5 fl oz semi-skimmed milk
2 eggs

BUTTER FILLING
25 g/1 oz cocoa powder
175 g/6 oz butter, softened
225 g/8 oz icing sugar + 1 tsp
a few drops vanilla extract

Five minute chocolate wonder

1 Grease and base-line 2 x 18 cm/7 in sandwich tins. Preheat the oven to 160°C/325°F/Gas 3.

2 Place all the ingredients for the cake in a food processor and blend together. When the mixture becomes smooth, dark and creamy, divide it between the 2 tins.

3 Bake for 25–35 minutes or until risen. Turn out onto wire racks to cool.

4 For the butter filling, mix the cocoa powder to a paste with a very little hot water. Leave to cool. Cream the butter in a bowl. Sift in the 225 g/8 oz icing sugar and a few drops of vanilla extract. Whisk really well until pale in colour and fluffy, then beat in the cocoa paste.

5 Sandwich the cooled cakes together with the butter filling. Sprinkle the top with a dusting of icing sugar.

Makes 9 squares
Prep time: 20 mins
Cook time: 1–1¹/₂ hours

250 g/9 oz plain flour
2 level tsp ground ginger
2 level tsp baking powder
1 level tsp bicarbonate of soda
50 g/1³/₄ oz cocoa powder

175 g/6 oz medium oatmeal
175 g/6 oz unsalted butter
175 g/6 oz dark soft brown sugar
300 g/10¹/₂ oz golden syrup
300 ml/10 fl oz semi-skimmed milk
1 egg, beaten
85 g/3 oz dark chocolate (min.
50–55% cocoa solids), chopped

Chocolate & ginger parkin

1 Grease and base-line a 23 cm/9 in square, deep cake tin.
Preheat oven to 180°C/350°F/Gas 4.

2 Sieve the first 5 dry ingredients together into a large
bowl. Stir in the oatmeal.

3 Meanwhile gently heat together the butter, sugar and
syrup in a saucepan until the sugar has dissolved. Whisk in
the milk and egg, then beat into the dry ingredients,
combining well to a smooth thick batter.

4 Fold in the chocolate. Pour into the tin and bake for
1–1¹/₂ hours or until firm to the touch but still slightly moist
in the middle when tested with the point of a knife. Leave
to cool in the tin before turning out onto a wire rack to
cool completely.

Serves 10–12
Prep time: 30 mins
Cook time: 40 mins

The alternative Christmas chocolate cake

100 g/3^1/$_2$ oz dark chocolate
(min. 70–75% cocoa solids)
150 ml/5 fl oz soured cream
175 g/6 oz unsalted butter
300 g/10^1/$_2$ oz soft brown sugar
zest of 2 oranges
3 eggs, beaten
300 g/10^1/$_2$ oz plain flour
2 tbsp cocoa powder
^{1}/$_2$ tsp baking powder
1^1/$_2$ tsp bicarbonate of soda

FILLING
300 g/10^1/$_2$ oz fresh cranberries
juice of 2 oranges
125 g/4^1/$_2$ oz caster sugar

FROSTING
2 egg whites
350 g/12 oz caster sugar
a good pinch of salt
juice of 1 lemon
^{1}/$_2$ tsp cream of tartar

DECORATION
foil-wrapped chocolate coins
whole physalis
cocoa powder, to dust

1 Grease and line a 23 cm/9 in spring-form cake tin. Preheat the oven to 180°C/350°F/Gas 4.

2 Heat the chocolate in a bowl set over a pan of gently simmering water. Remove from the pan and leave to cool a little. Stir in the soured cream.

continued next page

3 In a large bowl cream together the butter and brown sugar until pale and fluffy. Whisk in the orange zest, then the eggs, a little at a time, followed by the cooled chocolate and cream.

4 Sift on the remaining dry ingredients. Gently fold through to form a smooth batter. Pour into the tin and bake for 40 minutes or until risen and a skewer inserted into the centre comes out clean. Leave in the tin for 10 minutes before turning out onto a wire rack to cool.

5 Meanwhile make the filling: simmer the cranberries with the orange juice until the cranberries have softened and most of the fruit juice has evaporated. Stir in the sugar, leave to cool, then chill.

6 Now make the frosting: place all the ingredients in a large, grease-free bowl. Add 1 tablespoon of water. Set over a pan of gently simmering water and whisk with electric beaters for 10 minutes or until smooth and light. Remove from the pan and leave to cool, then cover with cling film until ready to use.

7 Split the chocolate cake in half horizontally and prick the lower half with a skewer. Spread the cranberries evenly over this and top with the other half.

8 Spread the frosting liberally over the top and sides of the cake. Leave to harden slightly, then decorate with coins and fruit and dust with cocoa powder.

Serves 8–10
Prep time: 15 mins
Cook time: 30–40 mins

100 g/3¹/₂ oz butter, diced
125 g/4¹/₂ oz dark chocolate
(min. 70–75 % cocoa solids)

6 eggs, separated
a pinch of salt
6 tbsp caster sugar
150 g/5¹/₂ oz ground almonds
whole almonds, to decorate
cocoa powder or icing sugar, for
dusting

Sunken gluten-free chocolate cake

1 Grease and base-line a 23 cm/9 in spring-form cake tin.
Preheat the oven to 160°C/325°F/Gas 3.

2 Melt the butter and chocolate together in a large,
heatproof bowl set over a pan of gently simmering water.
Remove from the pan and beat until smooth. Leave to cool
for 5 minutes, then beat in the egg yolks.

3 In a large clean bowl whisk the egg whites with a pinch of
salt until soft peaks form. Continue whisking, adding in the
sugar 1 tablespoon at a time, until the whites become stiff.
Stir 2 tablespoons of this into the chocolate mixture and stir
in the ground almonds, then carefully fold in the remainder
of the egg whites.

4 Dust the sides of the cake tin with a little cocoa powder to
help prevent sticking, then spoon in the mixture. Bake for
30–40 minutes or until well risen and just firm to touch.
Cool in the tin.

5 When ready to serve, decorate with whole almonds and
dust liberally with cocoa powder or icing sugar.

Makes 8 slices
Prep time: 15 mins
Cook time: 40–45 mins

175 g/6 oz butter
175 g/6 oz caster sugar
zest and juice of 2 oranges
2 tbsp milk

3 eggs
175 g/6 oz self-raising flour
1 tsp baking powder
75 g/2³/₄ oz good quality white chocolate, roughly chopped
¹/₂ tsp ground cinnamon (optional)
3 tbsp granulated sugar

White chocolate & orange drizzle cake

1 Grease and line a 900 g/2 lb loaf tin. Preheat the oven to 180°C/350°F/Gas 4.

2 In a large bowl cream together the butter, sugar and orange zest until light and fluffy. Whisk in the milk, then gradually beat in the eggs, one at a time with a spoonful of flour.

3 Fold in the remaining flour, baking powder, chocolate pieces and cinnamon, if liked.

4 Spoon into the tin, levelling the surface and bake for 40–45 minutes until well risen, golden and a skewer inserted into the centre comes out clean.

5 Meanwhile make the syrup: place the orange juice in a small saucepan and bring to the boil until reduced to 3 tablespoons. Leave to cool. Gently stir in the granulated sugar until it is just starting to absorb the juice and dissolve.

6 As soon as the cake comes out of the oven, prick it with a skewer several times and drizzle over the orange syrup. Leave the cake in the tin to cool completely before turning out.

Makes 16
Prep time: 15 mins
Cook time: 40 mins

175 g/6 oz dark chocolate
(min. 50–55% cocoa solids)
175 g/6 oz unsalted butter
225 g/8 oz light soft brown sugar

3 large eggs, beaten
85 g/3 oz plain flour
50 g/1¾ oz cocoa powder
½ tsp baking powder
200 g/7 oz full-fat cream cheese
a few drops of vanilla extract
1 tbsp icing sugar

Chocolate cheesecake swirls

1 Grease and base-line an 18 cm/7 in square baking tin,
5 cm/2 in deep. Preheat the oven to 180°C/350°F/Gas 4.

2 Gently melt together the chocolate, butter and brown sugar
in a large saucepan over a moderate heat. Stir until all
ingredients are smooth. Remove from the heat, leave to cool
slightly, then whisk in the eggs. Keep whisking until the
mixture is smooth.

3 Sift on the flour, cocoa powder and baking powder, folding
into the mixture. Pour into the tin.

4 Beat together the cream cheese, vanilla extract and icing
sugar. Dollop small spoonfuls over the chocolate mix then,
using a rounded knife, swirl the cream cheese through to
create a marbled effect.

5 Bake for 40 minutes or until just firm. Cool in the tin
before marking into squares.

Makes 16 squares
Prep time: 15 mins
Cook time: 30–40 mins

175 g/6 oz dark chocolate (min.
70–75% cocoa solids)
175 g/6 oz butter
3 eggs, beaten

200 g/7 oz caster sugar
a few drops natural vanilla extract
85 g/3 oz self-raising flour
25 g/1 oz cocoa powder + extra for
dusting
75 g/2³/₄ oz whole walnuts or pecan
nuts, coarsely chopped

Boston brownies

1 Lightly grease and line a 20 cm/8 in square baking tin,
5 cm/2 in deep, with parchment paper allowing a paper
collar 2.5 cm/1 in above the tin. Preheat the oven to
160°C/325°F/Gas 3.

2 Melt the chocolate and butter together in a large heatproof
bowl set over a pan of simmering water.

3 Remove the bowl from the heat and briskly stir in all the
remaining ingredients until well blended. Pour into the tin,
then bake for 30–40 minutes or until springy to the touch but
slightly soft in the centre.

4 Leave to cool in the tin for 2 hours, then turn out onto a
board. Cut into squares and dust with cocoa powder.

VARIATIONS
• Replace the nuts with chunks of white chocolate for a really
decadent brownie.
• For a thoroughly adult brownie, soak 50 g/2 oz pitted prunes
in brandy overnight, then fold in with chopped almonds
instead of walnuts at stage 3.

Makes 20
Prep time: 20 mins
Cook time: 50–60 mins

2 egg whites
50 g/1¾ oz caster sugar
50 g/1¾ oz icing sugar, sieved
2 level tbsp cocoa powder, sieved,
plus extra for dusting

FILLING
250 ml/9 fl oz whipping cream
1 tbsp icing sugar, sieved
75 g/2¾ oz dark or white chocolate,
finely grated

Chocolate kisses

1 Line 2 baking sheets with parchment. Preheat the oven to
140°C/275°F/Gas 1.

2 Whisk the egg whites in a clean bowl until they form soft
peaks. Very gradually whisk in the caster sugar, icing sugar
and cocoa powder until the meringue is really stiff and dry.

3 Spoon or pipe small whirls onto the baking sheets. Bake
for 50–60 minutes or until dry and crisp. Turn the
meringues over and leave in the turned-off oven to cool
completely. Store in an airtight container until required.

4 When ready to serve, whisk the cream until just stiffening,
then fold in the icing sugar and grated chocolate. Spoon a
small dollop of the cream onto half of the meringues, then
add the remaining halves and press lightly together. Dust
lightly with cocoa powder.

TIP
Do not sandwich
the meringues until
just ready to serve as
they will soften.

Makes 12
Prep time: 20 mins plus resting
Cook time: 12–15 mins

150 g/5¹/₂ oz icing sugar
3 rounded tbsp cocoa powder

150 g/5¹/₂ oz ground almonds or hazelnuts
3 egg whites
50 g/1³/₄ oz caster sugar
a few drops of vanilla extract

Chocolate macaroons

1 Line 2 large baking sheets with parchment. Preheat the oven to 160°C/325°F/Gas 3.

2 Make a stencil for the meringues by dipping the rim of a 4 cm/2 in pastry cutter in flour, then gently tapping onto the baking sheets. Mark out 12 circles, 2.5 cm/1 in apart.

3 Blend the icing sugar, cocoa powder and nuts in a food processor until very fine.

4 In a large clean bowl, whisk the egg whites until soft peaks form. Gradually add the caster sugar, whisking until the meringue is stiff and glossy. Fold in the ground nut mixture and the vanilla extract.

5 Gently spoon into a large disposable piping bag, snip off the bottom to make a 1 cm/³/₈ in hole, then pipe into rounds using the flour circles as a guide. Give the baking sheets a sharp rap to eliminate any air bubbles and leave to 'set' in a cool dry place for 30 minutes.

6 Bake one sheet at a time for 12–15 minutes or until they feel just firm, risen and glossy with a bubbled rim around the base. Cool on the sheets before carefully removing from the parchment paper.

Makes approx. 30
Prep time: 30 mins plus cooling
Suitable for freezing

250 g/9 oz dark chocolate (min.
70–75% cocoa solids)
150 ml/5 fl oz double cream

75 g/2¾ oz unsalted butter
2 tbsp rum or brandy
50 g/1¾ oz cocoa powder mixed
with a little icing sugar, for dusting
30–36 white paper sweet cases
(optional)

Rocky chocolate truffles

1 Gently melt the chocolate with the cream and butter in a
heatproof bowl set over a pan of simmering water.

2 Remove from the heat and stir in the rum or brandy. Beat
well until the mixture is shiny and smooth. Leave to cool
completely, cover and refrigerate for 3–4 hours or until the
mixture has firmed up enough to shape into truffles.

3 Have the paper cases ready on a tray or plate, if using. Sift
the cocoa powder and icing sugar onto a plate. Scoop half a
heaped teaspoon of truffle mix and toss into the cocoa powder
mix, then spoon into a case.

4 Store in the fridge for up to 3 days. They also freeze well.

VARIATION
For smooth, round truffles, dust your hands with cocoa
powder, then roll the mix into a small ball, roll it in the cocoa
powder and icing sugar, then place in a case. Work as quickly
as possible and do not over-roll the truffles.

Makes 12–16
Prep time: 10 mins
Cook time: 20–25 mins

225 g/8 oz butter
150 g/5¹/₂ oz light soft brown sugar
75 g/2³/₄ oz desiccated coconut
75 g/2³/₄ oz dried blueberries

50 g/1³/₄ oz cornflake cereal
2 tbsp cocoa powder
150 g/5¹/₂ oz self-raising flour
150 g/5¹/₂ oz white chocolate,
broken into pieces
150 g/5¹/₂ oz dark chocolate
(min. 50–55% cocoa solids),
broken into pieces

Chocolate, coconut & blueberry cereal bars

1 Base-line a 15 x 25 x 2.5 cm/6 x 10 x 1 in baking tin. Preheat the oven to 180°C/350°F/Gas 4.

2 In a large saucepan, melt the butter over a low heat. Stir in the sugar, coconut, blueberries and cornflakes. Gradually sift in the cocoa powder and flour. Mix together well.

3 Turn into the tin and level with a knife. Bake for 20–25 minutes. Leave in the tin, then cut into bars whilst still warm.

4 Meanwhile, melt the white and dark chocolate separately in heatproof bowls set over pans of simmering water. Spoon the melted plain chocolate in thick lines over the top of the tray bake, then fill in the gaps with the melted white chocolate. Use a palette knife to swirl the chocolates together to create a marbled effect. When the chocolate has just set, cut again into bars. Allow to cool completely before transferring to an airtight container.

Makes 20–24 small squares
Prep time: 15 mins
Cook time: 35 mins plus cooling

225 g/8 oz plain flour
75 g/2³/₄ oz caster sugar
150 g/5¹/₂ oz cold unsalted butter, diced

CARAMEL LAYER
125 g/4¹/₂ oz unsalted butter
125 g/4¹/₂ oz light soft brown sugar
1 x 397 g can condensed milk
a few drops of vanilla extract

CHOCOLATE TOPPING
200 g/7 oz dark or milk chocolate
1 tbsp vegetable oil

Millionaire's shortbread

1 Grease and base-line an 18 cm/7 in square cake tin, 5 cm/2 in deep. Preheat the oven to 180°C/350°F/Gas 4.

2 Mix together the flour and sugar in a large bowl. Rub in the cold butter until it resembles breadcrumbs, then knead the mixture to a smooth dough. Press the dough evenly into the tin. Prick all over with a fork. Bake for 20–25 minutes until light golden brown. Leave to cool.

3 For the caramel layer, melt the butter and sugar in a small pan over a gentle heat. Add the condensed milk. Stirring constantly, allow the mixture to come to a steady gentle simmer for 5 minutes. Remove from the heat, beat in the vanilla extract and pour over the shortbread. Leave to cool.

4 Melt the chocolate in a heatproof bowl set over a pan of simmering water. Stir in the vegetable oil, then spread over the cold caramel. Chill in the fridge until set. Cut into squares to serve.

VARIATION
Stir a handful of raisins or sultanas into the caramel topping.

Serves 8–10
Prep time: 40 mins plus chilling
Cook time: 20 mins

4 egg whites
250 g/9 oz caster sugar
1 tsp cornflour
1 tsp white wine vinegar
2 tsp coffee granules dissolved in
1 tbsp boiling water

FILLING
200 g/7 oz dark chocolate
(min. 70–75% cocoa solids),
broken into small pieces
600 ml/1 pt double cream
2 tbsp coffee liqueur or brandy
1 tbsp icing sugar
sifted cocoa powder, to decorate

Mocha mallow roulade

1 Line a 30 x 20 cm/12 x 8 in Swiss roll tin with baking parchment. Preheat the oven to 160°C/325°F/Gas 3.

2 Whisk the egg whites until stiff, then whisk in the caster sugar 1 tbsp at a time until stiff and shiny. Fold in the cornflour, vinegar and coffee, then spread gently into the tin. Bake for 20 minutes or until the surface is just crisp.

3 Leave to cool in the tin for a few minutes. Dust a piece of parchment paper slightly larger than the tin with icing sugar. Tip the meringue onto the paper, then ease away the lining.

4 Melt the chocolate in a heatproof bowl set over gently simmering water. Remove from the heat and leave to cool. Whip the cream and divide between 2 bowls. Reserve 5 tbsp of the chocolate, then fold the rest into 1 bowl of cream. Spread this over the roulade almost to the edges. Fold the liqueur and icing sugar into the other bowl and spread on top.

5 Starting from one short side, roll up the meringue. Place on a tray, seal side down, and refrigerate overnight to firm. To serve melt the reserved chocolate. Dust the roulade with cocoa powder, then drizzle over the chocolate.

Serves 6–8
Prep time: 20 mins
Cook time: 15–20 mins

50 g/1³/4 oz cocoa powder
150 g/5 oz organic dried apricots, chopped
200 ml/7 fl oz boiling water
a few drops of vanilla extract
1 tsp bicarbonate of soda
75 g/2³/4 oz unsalted butter

125 g/4¹/2 oz light muscovado sugar
2 eggs
175 g/6 oz self-raising flour

CHOC-ORANGE SAUCE
175 g/6 oz soft brown sugar
75 g/2³/4 oz unsalted butter
zest & juice of 1 orange
100 g/3¹/2 oz dark chocolate (min. 50–55% cocoa solids)
150 ml/5 fl oz double cream

Chocolate icky sticky with choc-orange sauce

1 Lightly grease eight 150 ml/5 fl oz pudding basins and dust with cocoa powder. Preheat the oven to 190°C/375°F/Gas 5.

2 Put the apricots in a bowl and pour over the boiling water. Add the vanilla and bicarbonate of soda and leave to one side.

3 Cream the butter and sugar together in a mixing bowl until light and fluffy. Gradually beat in the eggs, then add the flour, the remaining cocoa powder and the apricot mixture. Mix well. At this stage the mixture is very sloppy.

4 Pour the mixture into the basins and bake for 15-20 minutes or until the tops are set and the puddings have risen and shrunk from the sides. Turn out of the basins onto individual serving plates.

5 Meanwhile put all the sauce ingredients in a pan and heat gently, stirring occasionally, until the sugar is dissolved. Pour over the puddings.

Serves 6–8
Prep time: 25 mins
Cook time: 45–55 mins

250 g/9 oz butter
50 g/1³/₄ oz demerara sugar
6 whole blanched almonds
3 pears, peeled, halved & cored
175 g/6 oz caster sugar
2 large eggs

125 g/4¹/₂ oz self-raising flour
2 tbsp cocoa powder
50 g/1³/₄ oz ground almonds
2 tbsp milk

MILK CHOCOLATE SAUCE
75 g/2³/₄ oz milk chocolate (min.
50–55% cocoa solids), broken in
pieces
3 tbsp golden syrup
2 tbsp water

Chocolate & pear upside-down pudding

1 Grease and base-line a 25 cm/9 in deep, round, loose-bottomed cake tin. Preheat the oven to 180°C/350°F/Gas 4.

2 Melt 50 g/1³/₄ oz of the butter, mix with the demerara sugar and spread over the bottom of the cake tin.

3 Place an almond into each pear, then arrange the pears in the tin, cut side down and with stalk end toward the centre.

4 Cream the remaining butter with the caster sugar until light and fluffy. Beat in the eggs, 1 at a time, then fold in the flour, cocoa powder and ground almonds. If needed, add enough milk to form a soft dropping consistency. Spread the mixture evenly over the pears. Bake for 45–55 minutes or until the sponge springs back when lightly pressed.

5 To make the sauce, melt the chocolate with the syrup and water in a small heatproof bowl over a pan of simmering water, then beat until smooth. Turn the pudding out onto a serving dish, and pour over the warm chocolate sauce.

Makes 6
Prep time: 15 mins plus setting
Cook time: 14 mins

cocoa powder, for dusting
200 g/7 oz dark chocolate
(min.50–55% cocoa solids), broken
into pieces
150 g/5 oz butter, chopped + extra
for greasing

100 g/3¹/₂ oz caster sugar
3 eggs
3 egg yolks
1 tbsp dark rum (optional)
25 g/1 oz plain flour
whipped cream or icecream, to
serve

Chocolate fondant

1 Butter six 150 ml/5 fl oz dariole moulds well. Preheat the
oven to 200°C/400°F/Gas 6. Evenly coat the moulds with
sifted cocoa powder, tapping off any excess. Place the moulds
onto a baking sheet.

2 Gently heat together the chocolate, butter and sugar in a
heatproof bowl set over but not touching simmering water.
Once melted and the sugar no longer grainy, remove from the
heat and beat until smooth.

3 Add the eggs and egg yolks, one at a time, beating until
smooth and glossy. Add the rum if using and sift in the flour,
folding through gently.

4 Divide the mixture evenly between the moulds and place in
a fridge for at least 1 hour to set.

5 Cook for 14 minutes until risen and just setting on the
surface. Leave to stand for 2 minutes before carefully turning
out onto plates. Serve swiftly – with a generous dollop of
whipped cream or vanilla ice cream.

Serves 6
Prep time: 25 mins plus chilling
Cook time: 20 mins

4 eggs
75 g/2¾ oz caster sugar
25 g/1 oz ground walnuts
25 g/1 oz cocoa powder
25 g/1 oz plain flour
1–2 firm bananas

rum, to taste
300 ml/10 fl oz double cream
1 tbsp icing sugar

TO DECORATE
150 ml/5 fl oz double cream
50 g/1¾ oz dark chocolate (min.
50–55% cocoa solids), melted and
cut into triangles, see page 253
2 tsp icing sugar

Chocolate, walnut & banana roulade

1 Line a 30 x 20 cm/12 x 8 in Swiss roll tin. Preheat the oven to 190°C/375°F/Gas 5.

2 Whisk the eggs and sugar in a large bowl until thick and creamy. Lightly fold in the walnuts, cocoa powder and flour. Spread the mixture gently and evenly into the tin. Cook for approximately 20 minutes or until the sponge is golden and springs back when pressed. Turn out onto a lightly floured kitchen paper, roll up and leave to cool.

3 Slice the bananas thinly, then sprinkle with a little rum. Whisk the cream and icing sugar until thick.

4 Neaten the edges of the sponge, then unroll and spread on the cream almost to the edges. Scatter on the bananas and re-roll. Wrap in cling-film and chill until ready to serve.

5 Whisk the double cream to soft peaks. Pipe the cream along the top of the roulade, decorate with the chocolate triangles and dust with icing sugar.

Serves 6
Prep time: 20 mins
Cook time: 10 mins

melted butter, for greasing
50 g/1¾ oz caster sugar + extra for
dusting

175 g/6 oz dark chocolate (min.
50–55% cocoa solids) broken into
pieces
3 tbsp double cream
4 egg yolks
5 egg whites
icing sugar, for dusting

Hot chocolate soufflé

1 You will need six 150 ml/5 fl oz ramekin dishes and one
baking sheet. Preheat the oven to 200°C/400°F/Gas 6.

2 Place the baking sheet on the top shelf of the oven. Liberally
brush the ramekin dishes with melted butter, sprinkle each
with a teaspoon or so of the caster sugar, swirling to lightly
coat, then tipping out excess.

3 Melt the chocolate and cream in a large heatproof bowl set
over barely simmering water, cool, then whisk in the egg yolks.

4 Whisk the egg whites in another large clean bowl to soft
peaks, then whisk in the remaining sugar, a little at a time
until the egg whites are stiff. Whisk a spoonful into the
chocolate mixture, then gently fold in the remaining egg
whites.

5 Fill the ramekins, wipe the rims clean and run your thumb
around the edges. This helps the soufflé rise evenly. Place the
ramekins on the hot baking sheet and cook for 10–12 minutes
or until risen and slightly wobbly.

6 Dust sieved icing sugar over the top, then serve
straightaway.

Serves 8
Prep time: 30 mins
Cook time: 1–1¹/₂ hours

75 g/2³/₄ oz pistachio nuts, coarsely chopped
5 egg whites
250 g/9 oz caster sugar

100 g/3¹/₂ oz dark chocolate (min. 50–55% cocoa solids), chopped
100 g/3¹/₂ oz good quality white chocolate, chopped
100 g/3¹/₂ oz milk chocolate
450 ml/15 fl oz double cream
175 g/6 oz fresh raspberries
cocoa powder, for dusting

Triple chocolate pavlova

1 Line 2 baking sheets with baking parchment. Preheat the oven to 140°C/275°F/Gas 1. Draw a 23 cm/9 in circle on one sheet of parchment and a 15.5 cm/6 in circle on the other.

2 Dry-fry the nuts in a frying pan over a gentle heat. As soon as you smell a toasty aroma, remove from the heat to cool. Nuts burn very quickly!

3 Whisk the egg whites in a clean bowl until dry, then whisk in the sugar, a little at a time until glossy and stiff.

4 Gently fold in two-thirds of the nuts with the dark and white chocolate. Divide the meringue onto the parchment circles, spreading into peaked rounds. Bake for 1¹/₂ hours or until dry and the base sounds hollow when lightly tapped. Turn off the oven leaving the meringues to cool in the oven.

5 Meanwhile make some chocolate curls or shavings with the milk chocolate, see page 253.

6 To serve, lightly whip the cream and spread two-thirds over the large meringue. Scatter on half of the fruit, then top with the small meringue. Spread the remaining cream on top, then scatter over the remaining fruit, the chocolate shavings, a scattering of nuts and finally a dusting of cocoa powder.

Serves 6
Prep time: 10 mins
Cook time: 45–50 mins

100 g/3½ oz plain flour
2 level tsp baking powder

50 g/1¾ oz cocoa powder
150 g/5 oz granulated sugar
150 ml/5 fl oz single cream
a few drops of vanilla extract
75 g/2¾ oz demerara sugar
350 ml/12 fl oz boiling water

Puddle pudding

1 Lightly grease a 1.4 l/2½ pt ovenproof dish. Preheat the oven to 160°C/325°F/Gas 3.

2 Sift the flour, baking powder and 2 tablespoons of the cocoa powder into a bowl, then whisk in the granulated sugar, cream and vanilla extract. Beat well to a smooth batter.

3 Pour into the dish. Mix together the remaining cocoa powder with the demerara sugar and sprinkle evenly over the surface. Pour on the boiling water.

4 Bake for 40–45 minutes or until risen, slightly moist but firm to the touch. Divide between warm bowls, making sure everyone gets a generous spoonful of the hidden hot chocolate sauce.

TIP
Delicious with cold
pouring cream or
vanilla ice cream.

Serves 8–10
Prep time: 15 mins plus chilling
Cook time: 50–60 mins

100 g/3½ oz butter
250 g/9 oz plain shortbread or digestive biscuits, crushed

FILLING
175 g/6 oz white chocolate
375 g/13 oz cream cheese

75 g/2¾ oz caster sugar
a few drops vanilla extract
3 large eggs
200 ml/7 fl oz soured cream

TOPPING
75 g/2¾ oz caster sugar
150 ml/5 fl oz water
450 g/1 lb mixed summer berries
8–10 mint leaves, torn

White chocolate cheesecake

1 Base-line a 20 cm/8 in spring-form cake tin. Preheat the oven to 160°C/325°F/Gas 3.

2 Melt the butter in a bowl over a pan of barely simmering water. Stir in the biscuit crumbs, then spread into the tin, pressing down onto the base and sides. Chill for 5 minutes.

3 Melt the chocolate in a heatproof bowl over a pan of barely simmering water, stirring until smooth. Remove from the heat.

4 Whisk the cream cheese with the sugar and vanilla until smooth, then beat in the eggs, 1 at a time. Quickly stir the soured cream into the melted chocolate and add to the cream cheese mix, whisking until smooth. Pour over the biscuit base, level and bake for 50–60 minutes. Leave at room temperature for 1 hour, then chill until completely set.

5 For the topping, place the sugar and water in a pan and heat gently until dissolved; bring to the boil and simmer for a few minutes or until syrupy. Remove from the heat, then stir in the fruit and half the mint leaves. Leave to cool, then chill. Spoon over the cheesecake and decorate with remaining mint.

Serves 8–10
Prep time: 15 mins plus chilling
Cook time: 50–60 mins

50 g/1¾ oz butter, melted
200 g/7 oz pack chocolate-coated or
plain digestive biscuits, crushed

FILLING
150 g/5½ oz dark chocolate (min.
70–75% cocoa solids)

700 g/1lb 8 oz mascarpone cheese
125 g/4½ oz light soft brown sugar
2 tbsp cornflour
3 eggs, beaten
mini chocolate eggs, to decorate

WHITE CHOCOLATE SAUCE
125 g/4½ oz good quality white
chocolate
125 ml/4 fl oz double cream
15 g/½ oz butter

Baked cheesecake with white chocolate sauce

1 Base-line a 23 cm/9 in non-stick, spring-form cake tin. Preheat the oven to 180°C/350°F/Gas 4.

2 Melt the butter in a large bowl over a pan of barely simmering water. Stir in the crushed biscuits, then spread into the tin, pressing down evenly. Chill for 5 minutes.

3 Melt the dark chocolate in a small heatproof bowl set over the pan of barely simmering water. Stir until smooth, remove from heat and leave to cool a little.

4 In a large bowl, whisk together the mascarpone, sugar and cornflour until smooth. Whisk in the cooled chocolate and eggs. Spread over the biscuit base and level. Bake for 50–60 minutes. Turn off the oven and leave the door ajar until the cheesecake is completely cool. Decorate with mini eggs.

5 To make the sauce, place the white chocolate and cream in a small heatproof bowl set over a pan of simmering water. Heat until melted, then whisk in the butter.

Makes 8
Prep time: 40 mins plus chilling
Cook time: 20 mins

250 g/9 oz plain flour
125 g/4½ oz salted butter, cubed
3 tbsp caster sugar

FILLING
400 ml/14 fl oz milk
1 vanilla pod, split lengthways
3 egg yolks
25 g/1 oz cornflour
200 g/7 oz white chocolate
2–3 tbsp redcurrant jelly
150 ml/5 fl oz whipping cream
225 g/8 oz fresh strawberries

Chocolate & strawberry tarts

1 You will need 8 x 9 cm/3½ in round fluted tartlet tins. Preheat the oven to 200°C/400°F/Gas 6.

2 Rub the flour and butter together in a bowl until they resemble breadcrumbs. Stir in the sugar; add 2–3 tbsp cold water and work together to a soft dough. Chill for 30 minutes.

3 Gently heat the milk and vanilla pod in a pan until just scalding. In a large bowl beat together the egg yolks and cornflour. Strain on the milk whisking all the time. Discard the pod. Return to the pan, break in half the white chocolate. Stir constantly over a gentle heat until the chocolate has melted and the custard thickened. Set aside until cool.

4 Cut the pastry into 6; roll each to circles large enough to line the tins. Trim any excess. Line with paper and baking beans; bake blind for 15 minutes. Remove the beans and paper and bake for another 5 minutes. Transfer to a wire rack to cool.

5 Melt the remaining chocolate in a heatproof bowl set over gently simmering water, then brush over the pastry cases. Melt the redcurrant jelly. Whisk the cream to soft peaks, then fold into the custard. Divide between the tarts, arrange the strawberries on top and drizzle over the redcurrant jelly. Chill.

Serves 8–10

Prep time: 25 mins plus overnight soaking

Cook time: 33–45 mins

250 g/9 oz pitted ready-to-eat prunes, halved

3 tsp vanilla extract

175 g/6 oz butter

85 g/3 oz caster sugar

200 g/7 oz plain flour

50 g/1¾ oz cornflour

FILLING

100 g/3½ oz dark chocolate (min. 70–75% cocoa solids)

150 ml/5 fl oz double cream

2 tbsp caster sugar

250 g/9 oz mascarpone cheese

2 eggs, beaten

Dark chocolate, vanilla & prune tart

1 You will need a 23 cm/9 in deep fluted flan tin. Preheat the oven to 190°C/375°F/Gas 5.

2 Place the prunes in a bowl with the vanilla extract and 4 tbsp water. Stir to moisten thoroughly, then cover and leave in a cool place to soak overnight.

3 Cream the butter and sugar together, then work in both flours to a smooth firm dough. Place in the flan tin, pressing down evenly onto the base and sides. Chill for 15 minutes. Line the pastry case with greaseproof paper and fill with baking beans. Bake for 10–15 minutes, remove the beans and paper and bake for 3–5 minutes until just cooked. Reduce the oven temperature to 160°C/325°F/Gas 3.

4 Place the chocolate and cream in a heatproof bowl set over simmering water until the chocolate has just melted. Remove from the heat and whisk in the sugar, mascarpone and eggs.

5 Stir in the prunes and juices. Pour over the pastry case and bake for 20–25 minutes or until just set. Serve warm or chilled.

Serves 8
Prep time: 15 mins plus chilling
Cook time: 43–60 mins

175 g/6 oz butter
85 g/3 oz caster sugar
200 g/7 oz plain flour
50 g/1¾ oz cornflour

FILLING
200 g/7 oz dark chocolate
(min. 50–55% cocoa solids)
125 g/4½ oz unsalted butter
1 tbsp instant coffee dissolved in
1 tbsp boiling water
150 ml/5 fl oz single cream
175 g/6 oz dark soft brown sugar
3 eggs, beaten

Mississippi mud pie

1 You will need a 23cm/9 in deep fluted flan tin. Preheat the oven to 190°C/375°F/Gas 5.

2 Cream the butter and sugar together, then work in both flours to a smooth, firm dough. Press into the flan tin, lining it as evenly as possible. Chill for 15 minutes. Line the pastry case with greaseproof paper and fill with baking beans. Bake blind for 10–15 minutes, then remove the beans and paper and return to the oven for 3–5 minutes until just cooked. Reduce the oven temperature to 160°C/325°F/Gas 3.

3 Break the chocolate into a heatproof bowl set over gently simmering water, adding the butter and coffee. Stir until the chocolate has just melted. Remove from the heat and whisk in the cream, dark sugar and eggs.

4 Pour into the pastry base and return to the oven for 30–40 minutes until the filling is set. Serve at room temperature.

TIP
For an even richer filling, replace the dark soft brown sugar with muscovado sugar.

Muffins &
Cupcakes

Makes 9
Prep time: 15 mins
Cook time: 22-25 mins

225 g/8 oz plain flour
2 tsp baking powder
115 g/4 oz caster sugar

175 g/6 oz prepared fresh
blueberries
1 egg, beaten
115 g/4 oz butter or margarine,
melted
150 ml/5 fl oz whole milk
1 tsp pure vanilla extract

Blueberry muffins

1 Line a 9-hole muffin pan with large paper cases. Preheat the oven to 190°C/375°F/Gas 5.

2 Sift the flour and baking powder into a mixing bowl, then stir in the sugar and blueberries. Make a well in the centre.

3 In a measuring jug, mix together the egg, melted butter or margarine, milk and vanilla extract. Pour into the well and mix lightly to form a thick rough batter.

4 Spoon into the muffin cases and bake for 22–25 minutes, until risen and golden. Transfer to a wire rack to cool. Best served warm.

Makes 10
Prep time: 15 mins
Cook time: 25–28 mins

350 g/12 oz plain flour
1 tsp bicarbonate of soda
115 g/4 oz caster sugar
200 g/7 oz sultanas
2 eggs, beaten

115 g/4 oz butter or margarine, melted
150 ml/5 fl oz buttermilk
finely grated zest of 1 unwaxed lemon
100 ml/3$^{1}/_{2}$ fl oz freshly squeezed lemon juice
10 pieces pared lemon zest

Lemon and sultana muffins

1 Line a 10-hole muffin pan with very large paper cases. Preheat the oven to 190°C/375°F/Gas 5.

2 Sift the flour and bicarbonate of soda into a mixing bowl, then stir in the sugar and sultanas. Make a well in the centre.

3 In a measuring jug, mix together the egg, melted butter or margarine, buttermilk, lemon zest and juice. Pour into the well and mix lightly to form a thick rough batter.

4 Spoon into the muffin cases and place a piece of lemon zest on top. Bake for 25–28 minutes, until risen and golden. Transfer to a wire rack to cool completely.

TIP
For a flavour twist, replace lemon with orange zest and juice and use chopped, dried apricots instead of sultanas. Use a vegetable peeler to thinly pare off shavings of lemon zest for extra flavour and decoration.

Makes 12
Prep time: 20 mins
Cook time: 22–25 mins

400 g/14 oz plain flour
100 g/3½ oz butter or margarine
75 g/2½ oz + 1 tbsp caster sugar

1 tbsp baking powder
2 tsp ground cinnamon
2 eggs, beaten
150 ml/5 fl oz non-concentrated fresh apple juice
6 tbsp chunky apple sauce

Spiced apple sauce streusel muffins

1 Line a 12-hole muffin pan with large paper cases. Preheat the oven to 200°C/400°F/Gas 6.

2 Sift 50 g/2 oz of the flour into a bowl and rub in 25 g/1 oz of the butter or margarine to form a crumbly topping. Stir in 1 tbsp of the sugar and set aside. Melt the remaining butter or margarine.

3 Sift the remaining flour along with the baking powder and cinnamon into another bowl, then stir in the remaining sugar. Make a well in the centre.

4 In a measuring jug, mix together the eggs and melted butter or margarine with the apple juice and sauce. Pour into the well and mix lightly to form a thick rough batter.

5 Spoon into the muffin cases. Sprinkle the tops lightly with the crumble mix and bake for 22–25 minutes, until risen and lightly golden. Transfer to a wire rack to cool. Best served warm.

Makes 12
Prep time: 25 mins plus setting
Cook time: 16–18 mins

115 g/4 oz butter or baking margarine, softened
115 g/4 oz caster sugar

2 eggs, beaten
115 g/4 oz self-raising flour

ICING
175 g/6 oz icing sugar
assorted food colourings (optional)
sugar flowers, to decorate

Fairy cupcakes

1 Line a 12-hole cupcake pan with standard-size paper cases. Preheat the oven to 190°C/375°F/Gas 5.

2 In a mixing bowl, beat together the butter or margarine with the sugar until pale and creamy-light in texture.

3 Gradually whisk in the eggs, then sift the flour on top. Using a large metal spoon, carefully fold the flour into the batter.

4 Spoon into the cake cases and bake for 16–18 minutes until lightly golden and just firm to the touch. Transfer to a wire rack to cool completely.

5 To ice, sift the icing sugar into a bowl and gradually mix in sufficient warm water to make a smooth, spreadable icing. If using food colourings, divide into smaller bowls and mix in a few drops of your favourite shades.

TIP
For Chocolate Fairy Cakes, replace 15 g/1/2 oz of flour with cocoa powder and replace 15 g/1/2 oz icing sugar with cocoa powder to make a chocolate-flavoured icing.

6 Carefully spread the icing over each cake to cover, and decorate with sugar flowers. Allow to set for about 30 minutes before serving.

Makes 12
Prep time: 25 mins
Cook time: 16–18 mins

75 g/2¹/₂ oz butter or baking
margarine, softened
50 g/2 oz crunchy peanut butter
115 g/4 oz caster sugar
2 eggs, beaten
100 g/3¹/₂ oz self-raising flour

15 g/¹/₂ oz cocoa powder
100 g/3¹/₂ oz milk or plain
chocolate chips

TOPPING
125 g/4¹/₂ oz full-fat soft cheese
125 g/4¹/₂ oz chocolate spread,
softened
40 g/1¹/₂ oz peanut brittle, crushed

Peanut butter and chocolate cupcakes

1 Line a 12-hole cupcake pan with standard-size paper cases.
Preheat the oven to 190°C/375°F/Gas 5.

2 In a mixing bowl, beat together the butter or margarine
and peanut butter with the sugar until pale and creamy-light
in texture.

3 Gradually whisk in the eggs, then sift the flour and cocoa
powder on top. Add the chocolate chips, then, using a large
metal spoon, carefully fold the flour and chips into the batter.

4 Spoon into the cake cases and bake for 16–18 minutes until
lightly risen and just firm to the touch. Transfer to a wire rack
to cool.

5 For the topping, put the soft cheese in a bowl and beat until
softened. Add the chocolate spread and gently mix together to
give a marbled effect.

6 Just before serving, spread each cupcake thickly with the
chocolaty soft cheese and sprinkle with peanut brittle.

Makes 12
Prep time: 25 mins
Cook time: 16–18 mins

1 quantity Fairy Cupcake mixture,
see page 201
25 g/1 oz ground almonds
50 g/2 oz glacé cherries, chopped
1 tsp pure almond extract

TOPPING
icing sugar, to dust
125 g/4¹/₂ oz marzipan
4 tbsp cherry jam
fresh cherries, washed, to decorate
(see TIP)

Cherry almond cupcakes

1 Line a 12-hole cupcake pan with standard-size paper cases.
Preheat the oven to 190°C/375°F/Gas 5.

2 Make up the Fairy Cupcake mixture, see steps 2 and 3 on
page 201, then stir in the ground almonds, chopped cherries
and almond extract.

3 Spoon into the cake cases and bake for 16–18 minutes until
risen and lightly golden, and just firm to the touch. Transfer
to a wire rack to cool.

4 Dust the work surface lightly with icing sugar and roll out
the marzipan thinly. Using a 5 cm/2 in fluted round cutter,
stamp out 12 rounds, re-rolling as necessary.

5 Spoon cherry jam onto each cake and lay a circle of
marzipan on top. Decorate each with a fresh cherry.

TIP
To sugar-dip fresh cherries,
brush with lightly whisked
egg white, then dip in caster
sugar. Allow to dry for a few
minutes on baking
parchment.

Makes 10
Prep time: 25 mins
Cook time: 16–18 mins

115 g/4 oz butter or baking margarine, softened
115 g/4 oz caster sugar
1 tsp pure vanilla extract
2 eggs, beaten

115 g/4 oz plain flour
1¹/₂ tsp baking powder

ICING
75 g/2¹/₂ oz unsalted butter, softened
150 g/5 oz icing sugar + 1 tsp
¹/₂ tsp pure vanilla extract
assorted food colourings (optional)
short thin lengths of candied peel or angelica, to decorate

Butterfly cupcakes

1 Line a 10-hole cupcake pan with standard-size paper cases. Preheat the oven to 190°C/375°F/Gas 5.

2 In a mixing bowl, beat the butter with the sugar until pale and creamy-light in texture. Stir in the vanilla extract. Gradually whisk in the eggs, then sift the flour and baking powder on top and carefully fold into the batter.

3 Spoon into the cake cases and bake for 16–18 minutes until risen, lightly golden and just firm to the touch. Transfer to a wire rack to cool.

4 For the icing, place the butter in a bowl and beat until soft. Sift and beat in 150 g/5 oz of the icing sugar until smooth. Add vanilla to flavour. If using food colourings, divide into smaller bowls and mix in a few drops. Set aside.

5 Cut a circle off the top of each cake and cut in half. Spread half the icing onto the cakes. Put the rest in a piping bag filled with a 1 cm/¹/₂ in plain nozzle and pipe down the centre of each cake. Arrange 2 half circles on top to resemble wings. Dust with 1 tsp icing sugar and decorate with peel or angelica.

Makes 8
Prep time: 25 mins
Cook time: 22–25 mins

1 quantity Butterfly Cupcake
mixture, see page 206
50 g/2 oz dried strawberries,
chopped

TOPPING
5 tbsp strawberry jam
100 ml/3^1/$_2$ fl oz whipping cream
^{1}/$_2$ tsp pure vanilla extract
small fresh strawberries, halved,
to decorate

Strawberry and fresh cream cupcakes

1 Line an 8-hole muffin pan with large paper cases. Preheat the oven to 190°C/375°F/Gas 5.

2 Make up the Butterfly Cupcake mixture as directed in step 2 on page 206, then fold in the chopped, dried strawberries.

3 Spoon into the cake cases and bake for 22–25 minutes until risen and lightly golden, and just firm to the touch. Transfer to a wire rack to cool.

4 Using a teaspoon, carefully scoop out a circle about 2 cm/^{3}/$_4$ in deep from the top of each cake and reserve. Spoon a little strawberry jam into each of the cakes, then sit the reserved circle back on top.

5 Lightly whip the cream with the vanilla extract until just peaking. Transfer the cream to a piping bag fitted with a 1 cm/^{1}/$_2$ in star nozzle and pipe a swirl on top of each cake. Decorate with fresh strawberries and serve immediately.

Makes 10
Prep time: 20 mins plus standing
Cook time: 25–28 mins

265 g/9¹/₂ oz plain flour
2 tsp baking powder
40 g/1¹/₂ oz fine oatmeal, lightly toasted
125 g/4¹/₂ oz light brown sugar
200 g/7 oz prepared fresh raspberries

2 eggs, beaten
125 g/4¹/₂ oz butter or margarine, melted
200 ml/7 fl oz whole milk

SYRUP
50 g/2 oz caster sugar
approx. 4 tbsp Scotch whisky or freshly squeezed orange juice

Raspberry "Cranachan" muffins

1 Line a 10-hole muffin pan with very large paper cases. Preheat the oven to 190°C/375°F/Gas 5.

2 Sift the flour and baking powder into a mixing bowl, then stir in the oatmeal, sugar and raspberries. Make a well in the centre. In a measuring jug, mix together the eggs, melted butter or margarine and milk. Pour into the well and mix lightly to form a thick rough batter.

3 Spoon into the muffin cases and bake for 25–28 minutes, until risen and golden. Transfer to a wire rack.

4 Meanwhile, put the sugar in a small saucepan and pour over 150 ml/5 fl oz water. Stir over a low heat until dissolved, then raise the heat and boil for 3–4 minutes until syrupy. Remove from the heat, cool slightly, then stir in whisky or orange juice to taste.

5 Prick the hot muffins with a fork and spoon a little syrup over each. Stand for 30 minutes before serving.

Makes 10
Prep time: 15 mins plus cooling
Cook time: 23–25 mins

350 g/12 oz plain flour
1 tsp bicarbonate of soda
115 g/4 oz pecan nuts, finely chopped

1 large egg, beaten
200 ml/7 fl oz buttermilk
125 ml/4$^{1/2}$ fl oz maple syrup
100 ml/3$^{1/2}$ fl oz sunflower oil
10 pecan halves

Pecan and maple muffins

1 Line a 10-hole muffin pan with large paper cases. Preheat the oven to 190°C/375°F/Gas 5.

2 Sift the flour and bicarbonate of soda into a mixing bowl. Stir in the chopped pecans. Make a well in the centre.

3 In a measuring jug, mix together the egg, buttermilk, 100 ml/3$^{1}/_{2}$ fl oz of the maple syrup and the oil. Pour into the well and mix lightly to form a thick rough batter.

4 Spoon into the muffin cases, put a pecan half on top of each and bake for 23–25 minutes, until risen and lightly golden. Transfer to a wire rack and brush with remaining maple syrup to glaze. Best served warm.

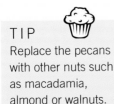
TIP
Replace the pecans with other nuts such as macadamia, almond or walnuts.

Makes 12
Prep time: 20 mins
Cook time: 16–18 mins

40 g/1½ oz plain chocolate-coated
coffee beans
1 quantity Fairy Cupcake mixture,
see page 201

TOPPING
150 ml/5 fl oz whipping cream
2 tsp drinking chocolate powder
12 small coffee bean-shaped
chocolates (also called *chicchi
di caffe*)

Cappuccino cupcakes

1 Line a 12-hole cupcake pan with standard-size paper cases. Preheat the oven to 190°C/375°F/Gas 5.

2 Grind the chocolate-coated coffee beans in a coffee grinder or blender until fine and well ground.

3 Make up the Fairy Cupcake mixture as directed in steps 2 and 3 on page 201, then carefully stir in the ground coffee beans.

4 Spoon into the cake cases and bake for 16–18 minutes until lightly risen and just firm to the touch. Transfer to a wire rack to cool.

5 Lightly whip the cream until just peaking. Spoon on top of each cupcake to resemble the frothy milk on top of a cup of coffee. Dust lightly with drinking chocolate and decorate with a chocolate bean.

Makes 10
Prep time: 25 mins plus setting
Cook time: 16–18 mins

1 quantity plain Butterfly Cupcake
mixture, see page 206 and below
50 g/2 oz finely grated fresh coconut
finely grated zest 1 lime

ICING
150 g/5 oz icing sugar
juice 1 lime
a few drops green food colouring
(optional)
50 g/2 oz piece fresh coconut
lime zest, to decorate

Fresh coconut and lime cupcakes

1 Line a 10-hole cupcake pan with standard-size paper cases. Preheat the oven to 190°C/375°F/Gas 5.

2 Make up the Butterfly Cupcake mixture as directed in step 2 on page 206 but omitting the vanilla extract, then carefully stir in the finely grated coconut together with the lime zest.

3 Spoon into the cake cases and bake for 16–18 minutes until risen and lightly golden, and just firm to the touch. Transfer to a wire rack to cool.

4 Sift the icing sugar into a bowl and gradually mix in sufficient lime juice to make a smooth, spreadable icing. Add a few drops of food colouring if liked.

5 Spread some of the lime icing over each cupcake. Using a vegetable peeler, shave off small pieces of coconut on top of each cake. Stand for a few minutes for the icing to set before serving decorated with lime zest.

TIP
For a more intense coconut flavour, use unsweetened desiccated coconut instead of fresh.

Makes 44
Prep time: 40 mins plus cooling
Cook time: 12–14 mins

115 g/4 oz 70% cocoa dark
chocolate, broken into pieces
125 g/4½ oz butter
100 g/3½ oz caster sugar
2 eggs, beaten
50 g/2 oz self-raising flour
1 tsp baking powder

1 tsp ground cinnamon
1 tsp ground allspice
50 g/2 oz ground almonds
1 tsp finely grated orange zest

GANACHE-STYLE ICING
225 g/8 oz plain chocolate, broken
into pieces
250 ml/9 fl oz double cream, at
room temperature
edible gold leaf, to decorate

Mini mayan gold cupcakes

1 Line 44-hole mini muffin pans with mini muffin paper cases. Preheat the oven to 180°C/350°F/Gas 4.

2 Put the chocolate and butter into a heatproof bowl and place over a saucepan of barely simmering water to melt. Remove from the water and stir in the sugar. Set aside for 10 minutes.

3 Gradually whisk the eggs into the chocolate mixture to make a thick, glossy batter. Sift the flour, baking powder and spices on top, then add the ground almonds and orange zest. Using a large metal spoon, carefully fold into the cake batter.

4 Spoon into the cake cases to almost fill them and bake for 12–14 minutes until lightly risen and just firm to the touch. Transfer to a wire rack to cool.

5 For the icing, melt the chocolate as above, then cool until only slightly warm. Whisk while slowly pouring in the cream. Continue whisking until glossy. Immediately, spoon into a piping bag fitted with a 1 cm/½ in star nozzle and pipe a swirl onto each cupcake. Just before serving, add a piece of gold leaf.

Makes 8
Prep time: 25 mins plus cooling
Cook time: 22–25 mins

1 quantity Fairy Cupcake mixture,
see page 201
1 tsp finely grated lemon zest
150 g/5 oz good quality lemon curd

TOPPING
115 g/4 oz crème fraîche
8 mini meringues
strips of lemon zest

Lemon meringue cupcakes

1 Line an 8-hole muffin pan with large paper cases. Preheat
the oven to 190°C/375°F/Gas 5.

2 Make up the Fairy Cupcake mixture as directed in steps
2 and 3 on page 201, then carefully stir in the lemon zest.

3 Half-fill each cake case with the lemon cake mixture.
Spoon a generous teaspoon of lemon curd on top, then cover
with the remaining cake mixture. Bake for 22–25 minutes
until risen and lightly golden, and just firm to the touch.
Transfer to a wire rack to cool.

4 When ready to serve, spoon a generous dollop of
crème fraîche on top of each cake, then some of the
remaining lemon curd. Prop a mini meringue on top and
decorate with lemon zest. Serve immediately.

Makes 8
Prep time: 25 mins
Cook time: 22–25 mins

115 g/4 oz unsalted butter, softened
115 g/4 oz light brown sugar
1 tsp pure vanilla extract
2 eggs, beaten
115 g/4 oz plain flour

1½ tsp baking powder
100 g/3½ oz mini fudge pieces

ICING
75 g/3 oz unsalted butter, softened
150 g/5 oz icing sugar
4 tbsp caramel filling (also called
dulce de leche)

Sticky toffee cupcakes

1 Line an 8-hole muffin pan with large paper cases. Preheat the oven to 190°C/375°F/Gas 5.

2 In a mixing bowl, beat the butter with the sugar until pale, and creamy-light in texture. Stir in the vanilla extract.

3 Gradually whisk in the eggs, then sift the flour and baking powder on top. Add all but 25 g/1 oz of the fudge pieces, then, using a large metal spoon, carefully fold into the cake batter.

4 Spoon into the cake cases and bake for 22–25 minutes until lightly risen and lightly golden, and just firm to the touch. Transfer to a wire rack to cool.

5 For the icing, place the butter in a bowl and beat until soft. Gradually sift and beat in the icing sugar to make a smooth, creamy icing. Beat in the caramel filling.

6 Pile the icing into a piping bag fitted with a 1 cm/½ in star nozzle. Pipe a generous swirl on top of each cake and sprinkle with the remaining fudge pieces to serve.

Makes 12
Prep time: 15 mins
Cook time: 22–25 mins

225 g/8 oz wholewheat plain flour
2 tsp baking powder
115 g/4 oz light brown sugar
115 g/4 oz breakfast muesli

1 egg, beaten
115 g/4 oz butter or margarine, melted
200 ml/7 fl oz whole milk
1 large ripe banana, peeled and mashed
1 tsp pure vanilla extract
12 dried banana chips

Breakfast muesli and banana muffins

1 Line a 12-hole muffin pan with large paper cases. Preheat the oven to 190°C/375°F/Gas 5.

2 Sift the flour and baking powder into a mixing bowl, adding any husks that remain in the sieve. Stir in the sugar and muesli. Make a well in the centre.

3 In a measuring jug, mix together the egg, melted butter or margarine, milk, banana and vanilla extract. Pour into the well and mix lightly to form a thick rough batter.

4 Spoon into the muffin cases, put a banana chip on top of each and bake for 22–25 minutes, until risen and lightly golden. Transfer to a wire rack to cool. Best served warm.

Makes 12
Prep time: 15 mins
Cook time: 22–25 mins

50 g/2 oz + 2 tbsp porridge oats
225 g/8 oz wholewheat plain flour
2 tsp baking powder
200 g/7 oz prepared fresh
blackberries

1 egg, beaten
115 g/4 oz butter or margarine,
melted
150 ml/5 fl oz whole milk
115 g/4 oz strong-flavoured honey,
such as heather

Bramble, honey and oat muffins

1 Line a 12-hole muffin pan with large paper cases. Preheat the oven to 190°C/375°F/Gas 5.

2 Put 50 g/2 oz of the oats in a bowl and sift the flour and baking powder on top, adding any husks that remain in the sieve. Stir in the blackberries. Make a well in the centre.

3 In a measuring jug, mix together the egg, melted butter or margarine and milk. Pour into the well, add the honey and mix lightly to form a thick rough batter.

4 Spoon into the muffin cases and sprinkle each lightly with the remaining oats. Bake for 22–25 minutes, until risen and golden. Transfer to a wire rack to cool. Best served warm.

Makes 9
Prep time: 15 mins
Cook time: 20 mins

150 g/5 oz spelt or wholewheat flour
1 tbsp baking powder
salt and freshly ground black pepper
150 g/5 oz polenta or fine cornmeal
3 eggs, beaten

200 ml/7 fl oz whole milk
150 g/5 oz goats' cheese, crumbled or grated
50 g/2 oz dry pack sun-dried tomatoes, soaked and finely chopped
1 tbsp freshly chopped rosemary or 2 tsp dried
9 small sprigs fresh rosemary, to garnish
sweet tomato chutney, to serve

Goat's cheese and tomato muffins

1 Grease a 9-hole muffin pan well or use a silicone muffin pan. Preheat the oven to 190°C/375°F/Gas 5.

2 Sift the flour, baking powder and seasoning into a bowl and add any wheat husks that remain in the sieve. Stir in the polenta and make a well in the centre.

3 Add the eggs and milk. Gradually mix together to form a smooth batter. Stir in the remaining ingredients except the garnish and chutney.

4 Spoon into the muffin pan and bake for about 20 minutes, until risen, golden and firm to the touch. Transfer to a wire rack to cool. Best served warm. Garnish with fresh rosemary and serve split and filled with sweet tomato chutney.

TIP
Spelt flour is made from an ancient wheat grain *Triticum spelta*, used in Roman times. It is a light wholewheat flour with a lower gluten content than other wheat flours and makes a delicious soft-textured muffins & cupcakes cake mixture.

Makes 12
Prep time: 30 mins plus cooling and setting
Cook time: 22–24 mins

40 g/1½ oz 85% cocoa dark chocolate, broken into pieces
190 g/6½ oz dark brown sugar, free of lumps
40 g/1½ oz unsalted butter, softened

2 eggs, separated
225 g/8 oz peeled chestnuts, finely ground

ICING
150 g/5 oz icing sugar
1 tsp liquid coffee essence
chocolate curls, to decorate

Mocha chestnut cupcakes

1 Line a 12-hole cupcake pan with standard-size paper cases. Preheat the oven to 180°C/350°F/Gas 4.

2 Put the chocolate in a saucepan with the sugar and butter, and place over a gentle heat to melt, stirring occasionally until thick. Transfer to a heatproof bowl and cool for 10 minutes.

3 Place the egg whites in a large, grease-free bowl. Whisk until stiff.

4 Beat the egg yolks into the chocolate, then fold in the ground chestnuts. Mix a quarter of the egg whites into the mixture to loosen it, then carefully fold in the remainder.

5 Spoon into the cake cases and bake for 22–24 minutes until lightly risen and just firm to the touch. Transfer to a wire rack to cool.

6 For the icing, sift the icing sugar into a bowl. Add the coffee essence and gradually mix in sufficient warm water to make a smooth icing. Carefully spread the icing over each cake and sprinkle with chocolate curls to decorate. Allow to set for about 30 minutes before serving.

Makes 30
Prep time: 20 mins
Cook time: 12 mins

225 g/8 oz spelt or wholewheat flour
2 tsp baking powder
1 tsp smoked paprika + extra to dust

salt and freshly ground black pepper
75 g/2¹/₂ oz cooked smoked bacon, finely chopped
75 g/2¹/₂ oz freshly grated Parmesan cheese
2 eggs, beaten
200 ml/7 fl oz whole milk

Smoky bite-sized cheese and bacon muffins

1 Line 30-hole mini muffin pans with mini muffin paper cases. Preheat the oven to 200°C/400°F/Gas 6.

2 Sift the flour, baking powder, smoked paprika and seasoning into a bowl and add any wheat husks that remain in the sieve. Stir in the bacon and cheese. Make a well in the centre.

3 Add the eggs and milk. Gradually mix together to form a smooth batter.

4 Spoon the mixture into the muffin cases to fill them and bake for about 12 minutes, until risen, and just firm to the touch. Transfer to a wire rack to cool. Best served warm, dusted with extra paprika.

TIP
Smoked paprika adds a delicious sweet-smoke flavour to baking; varieties can be mild or hot. Use plain sweet paprika or regular chilli powder if preferred.

Makes 9
Prep time: 25 mins
Cook time: 20 mins

115 g/4 oz plain flour
2 tsp baking powder
1/2 tsp bicarbonate of soda
150 g/5 oz yellow cornmeal
or polenta
3 tbsp caster sugar
1 egg, beaten

225 ml/8 fl oz buttermilk
50 g/2 oz butter or margarine,
melted
2 spring onions, trimmed and finely
chopped
50 g/2 oz cooked red pepper, finely
chopped
50 g/2 oz cooked sweetcorn kernels
salt and freshly ground black pepper
1–2 tsp dried chilli flakes, to taste
9 slices jalapeño pepper

Mexican cornbread muffins

1 Line a 9-hole muffin pan with large paper cases. Preheat the oven to 190°C/375°F/Gas 5.

2 Sift the flour, baking powder and bicarbonate of soda into a mixing bowl and stir in the cornmeal and sugar. Make a well in the centre.

3 Add the egg, buttermilk and melted butter or margarine Gently mix together to form a smooth batter. Stir in the onions, peppers, sweetcorn, seasoning and chilli flakes to taste.

4 Spoon into the muffin cases and place a slice of jalapeño on top of each. Bake for about 20 minutes, until risen, golden and firm to the touch. Transfer to a wire rack to cool. Best served warm.

TIP
Use cornmeal if you can, as it is often more finely ground than polenta.

Makes 9
Prep time: 20 mins
Cook time: 18–20 mins

115 g/4 oz butter or vegetable
margarine, softened
115 g/4 oz caster sugar
finely grated zest 1 lemon
2 eggs, beaten
75 g/2½ oz spelt flour
1 tsp baking powder

50 g/2 oz ground almonds
2 tbsp poppy seeds
25 g/1oz pumpkin seeds, chopped

SYRUP AND TOPPING
50 g/2 oz caster sugar
juice 1 lemon made up to
150 ml/5 fl oz with cold water
200 g/7 oz soft cheese
4 tbsp good quality lemon curd
lemon jelly slices, to decorate

Seeded lemon cupcakes

1 Line a 9-hole cupcake pan with home-made (see page 12) or tulip baking cases. Preheat the oven to 190°C/375°F/Gas 5.

2 In a mixing bowl, beat the butter or margarine with the sugar until pale and creamy. Stir in the lemon zest. Gradually whisk in the eggs, then sift the flour and baking powder on top, adding any husks that remain in the sieve. Add the ground almonds and seeds, then fold into the batter.

3 Spoon into the cake cases and bake for 18–20 minutes until slightly risen, lightly golden and just firm to the touch. Leave in the cake pan.

4 To make the syrup. Put the sugar and diluted lemon juice in a small saucepan. Stir over a low heat until dissolved, then raise the heat and boil for 3–4 minutes until syrupy. Prick the hot cupcakes with a fork and spoon a little syrup over each. Stand for 10 minutes before transferring to a wire rack to cool.

5 To serve, mix the soft cheese and lemon curd together and spoon on top of each cupcake. Decorate with lemon jelly slices.

Makes 8
Prep time: 25 mins plus setting
Cook time: 10–12 mins

50 g/2 oz plain flour
75 g/2½ oz caster sugar
3 large egg whites
½ tsp cream of tartar
½ tsp pure vanilla extract

ICING
150 g/5 oz icing sugar
pinch dried lavender, finely ground
lilac food colouring
sugared lavender flowers,
to decorate

Angelic lavender cupcakes

1 Line an 8-hole muffin pan with large paper cases. Preheat the oven to 180°C/350°F/Gas 4.

2 Sift the flour and half the caster sugar into a small bowl.

3 In a large, grease-free bowl, whisk the egg whites until softly peaking but not stiff. Add the cream of tartar, remaining sugar and the vanilla extract. Continue whisking until thick and glossy. Sift in the flour and sugar mix, folding in gently after each addition until well combined.

4 Spoon the mixture into the cake cases to fill them and bake for 10–12 minutes until very lightly golden and slightly springy to the touch. Transfer to a wire rack to cool.

5 To ice, sift the icing sugar into a bowl. Add the ground lavender and gradually mix in sufficient warm water to make a smooth icing. Mix in a few drops of food colouring.

6 Spread the icing over each cake and decorate with lavender flowers. Allow to set.

TIP
To make the flowers, lightly brush small dried flowerheads of lavender with lightly beaten egg white, then dip in caster sugar. Leave to dry on a sheet of baking parchment.

Makes 9
Prep time: 15 mins
Cook time: 22–25 mins

115 g/4 oz plain flour
2 tsp baking powder
115 g/4 oz ground almonds
115 g/4 oz light brown sugar
115 g/4 oz dried cranberries

115 g/4 oz golden marzipan, cut into small pieces
1 egg, beaten
50 g/2 oz butter or margarine, melted
175 ml/6 fl oz whole milk
9 short lengths of festive ribbon, to decorate

Festive cranberry and marzipan muffins

1 Line a 9-hole muffin pan with large paper cases. Preheat the oven to 190°C/375°F/Gas 5.

2 Sift the flour and baking powder into a mixing bowl, then stir in the ground almonds, sugar, cranberries and chopped marzipan. Make a well in the centre.

3 In a measuring jug, mix together the egg, melted butter or margarine and milk. Pour into the well and mix lightly to form a thick rough batter.

4 Spoon into the muffin cases and bake for 22–25 minutes, until risen and golden. Transfer to a wire rack to cool a little. Best served warm. Tie with festive ribbon before serving.

Makes 8
Prep time: 15 mins
Cook time: 22–25 mins

225 g/8 oz plain flour
2 tsp baking powder
2 tsp mixed spice
115 g/4 oz light brown sugar
175 g/6 oz luxury dried fruit mix

1 egg, beaten
50 g/2 oz butter or margarine, melted
175 ml/6 fl oz whole milk

TOPPING
icing sugar, to dust
175 g/6 oz piece golden marzipan
2 tbsp apricot jam, sieved

Hot cross bun muffins

1 Line an 8-hole muffin pan with large paper cases. Preheat the oven to 190°C/375°F/Gas 5.

2 Sift the flour, baking powder and spice into a mixing bowl, then stir in the sugar and dried fruit. Make a well in the centre.

3 In a measuring jug, mix together the egg, melted butter or margarine and milk. Pour into the well and mix lightly to form a rough batter.

4 Spoon into the muffin cases and bake for 22–25 minutes, until risen and golden. Transfer to a wire rack to cool. Best served warm.

5 To finish, lightly dust the work surface with icing sugar and roll out the marzipan thinly to form a rectangle 20 x 10 cm/8 x 4 in. Cut into 16 thin strips. Brush the tops of the muffins with a little jam and secure a marzipan cross on top.

Makes 10
Prep time: 25 mins plus setting
Cook time: 16–18 mins

1 quantity Fairy Cupcake mixture,
see page 201
2 tsp ground cinnamon
1 tsp finely grated lemon zest

TOPPING
150 g/5 oz ricotta cheese
75 g/2¹/2 oz icing sugar
a few drops of pink food colouring
sugar flowers, to decorate

Spring flower power cupcakes

1 Line a 10-hole cupcake pan with standard-size paper cases.
Preheat the oven to 190°C/375°F/Gas 5.

2 Make up the Fairy Cupcake mixture as directed in steps
2 and 3 on page 201, then carefully stir in the ground
cinnamon and lemon zest.

3 Spoon into the cake cases and bake for 16–18 minutes until
lightly risen and lightly golden, and just firm to the touch.
Transfer to a wire rack to cool.

4 For the topping, put the ricotta cheese in a piping bag fitted
with a 1 cm/¹/2 in star nozzle. Take a sharp knife and cut a
circle off the top of each cake about 4 cm/1¹/2 inch in
diameter. Using either a small knife or flower-shaped cutter,
form each sponge circle into a flower shape. Pipe a swirl of
ricotta cheese on top of each of the cut cakes.

5 Sift the icing sugar into a small bowl and gradually mix in
sufficient warm water to make a smooth, spreadable icing. Add
a few drops of pink food colouring. Carefully spread each of
the flower cut-out tops with pink icing and sit on top of each
cupcake. Decorate with sugar flowers and allow to set.

Makes 16
Prep time: 50 mins plus chilling
Cook time: 33 mins (for cup cakes plus gingerbread)

FOR THE GINGERBREAD PEOPLE
125 g/4½ oz butter or margarine, softened
125 g/4½ oz dark brown sugar

1 large egg yolk
250 g/9 oz self-raising flour
1 tbsp ground ginger
assorted tubes of ready-made coloured piping icing
small sugar cake decorations

2 batches iced Sticky Toffee Cupcakes, see page 222

Little party people cupcakes

1 Line 2 large baking sheets with baking parchment. Preheat the oven to 180°C/350°F/Gas 4.

2 To make the gingerbread people, in a mixing bowl, beat the butter or margarine with the sugar until paler and creamy-light in texture. Stir in the egg yolk.

3 Gradually sift in the flour and ginger, beating well after each addition, to form a soft, crumbly mixture. Bring the mixture together with your hands and gently knead it on a lightly floured work surface until smooth. Wrap and chill for at least 2 hours – preferably overnight.

4 Roll the dough out thinly on a lightly floured work surface. Using mini gingerbread people cutters, stamp out as many people as you can, re-rolling the dough as necessary. The mixture should make about 50. Arrange on the baking sheets, prick each with a fork and bake for about 8 minutes until lightly golden and just firm. Allow to cool on the baking sheets.

5 To serve, decorate each little person, stand one on top of each cupcake and serve the rest separately.

Makes 10
Prep time: 35 mins
Cook time: 16–18 mins

1 quantity Butterfly Cupcake
mixture, see page 206

TOPPING
3 tbsp raspberry jam
1 quantity ganache-style icing made
with white chocolate, see page 218
10 birthday cake candles
assorted mini sweets, such as Jelly
Beans, Dolly Mixtures, to decorate

Birthday cupcakes

1 Line a 10-hole cupcake pan with standard-size paper cases.
Preheat the oven to 190°C/375°F/Gas 5.

2 Make up the Butterfly Cupcake mixture as directed in
step 2 on page 206.

3 Spoon into the cake cases and bake for 16–18 minutes until
lightly risen and lightly golden, and just firm to the touch.
Transfer to a wire rack to cool.

4 Using a teaspoon, carefully scoop out a circle about
2 cm/3/4 in deep from the top of each cake and set aside.
Spoon a little raspberry jam into each of the cakes and gently
push the reserved sponge circle back on top.

5 Make up the white chocolate ganache as described in step 5
on page 218 and immediately spoon into a piping bag fitted
with a 1 cm/1/2 in star nozzle and pipe a swirl on top of each
cupcake. Note: once cool the icing will set firm.

6 Push a cake candle into the top of each cake and decorate
with sweets before the ganache sets.

Makes 10
Prep time: 25 mins
Cook time: 16–18 mins

1 quantity Butterfly Cupcake
mixture, see page 206
50 g/2 oz dried sour cherries,
chopped
a few drops pink food colouring

TOPPING
5 tbsp cherry jam
150 ml/5 fl oz whipping cream
1/2 tsp pure almond extract
1 tbsp icing sugar, to dust

Sweetheart cupcakes

1 Line a 10-hole cupcake pan with standard-size paper cases.
Preheat the oven to 190°C/375°F/Gas 5.

2 Make up the Butterfly Cupcake mixture as directed in step 2
on page 206, then carefully stir in the chopped dried cherries
and a few drops of pink food colouring.

3 Spoon into the cake cases and bake for 16–18 minutes until
lightly risen and lightly golden, and just firm to the touch.
Transfer to a wire rack to cool.

4 Take a sharp knife and cut a circle off the top of each cake
about 4 cm/1 1/2 in in diameter. Using either a small knife or
heart-shaped cutter, form each sponge circle into a heart shape.

5 Using a teaspoon, carefully scoop out a little sponge from the
top of each cake and fill with a little cherry jam.

6 Lightly whip the cream with the almond extract until just
peaking. Transfer the cream to a piping bag fitted with a
1 cm/1/2 in star nozzle and pipe a swirl on top of each cake.

7 Sit the cake heart back on top of each cake at an angle; dust
lightly icing sugar and serve straightaway.

Basic methods

Icings, frostings and fillings
Quantities of each are enough for an average size cake.

Glacé icing
This simple icing has a sweet taste that can be sharpened with a little orange or lemon zest and juice.

225 g/8 oz icing sugar
3–4 tbsp water

Sieve the icing sugar into a bowl and stir in enough water to give a smooth icing that will coat the back of the spoon in a thick layer. A few drops of vanilla, almond or peppermint flavouring, food colouring or fruit syrups, such as grenadine, can also be stirred in. Use immediately as the icing will quickly form a crust.

Flavoured glacé icings
Citrus: replace the water with fresh lemon, orange or lime juice
Chocolate: replace 1 tablespoon of the icing sugar with cocoa powder
Coffee: replace the water with cold strong black coffee
Grown-up: replace the water with rum, brandy, Tia Maria, orange Curaçao, limoncello or similar

Buttercream
Creamy and sweet, the proportion of sugar to butter can be varied according to personal taste.

175 g /6 oz unsalted butter, softened
225 g/8 oz icing sugar
1 tbsp milk

Beat the butter in a bowl until creamy. Sieve in the icing sugar, a little at a time, beating well after each addition. Stir in the milk to soften. A few drops of food colouring can also be added. Use immediately or press cling film over the surface to prevent a crust from forming and keep refrigerated.

Flavoured buttercreams
Coffee: stir in 1 tbsp cold strong black coffee
Vanilla: stir in 1 tsp vanilla essence
Orange/Lemon: beat in the grated zest of 1 small orange or 1 lemon

Marshmallow frosting
A sweet, foamy favourite. Best used on a plain cake that is not too sweet.

275 g/10 oz granulated sugar
2 large egg whites
4 tbsp cold water
1 tbsp light corn syrup or runny honey
$\frac{1}{4}$ tsp cream of tartar

Whisk all the ingredients together in a large heatproof bowl until the sugar dissolves. Stand the bowl over a pan of simmering water (without letting the bottom of the bowl touch the water) and, using an electric hand whisk, beat on medium speed until fluffy – this will take about 4 minutes. Turn up the speed to high and continue to whisk until very thick – about 3 minutes. Remove the bowl to the work surface and keep whisking until the base of it is cold. Use immediately.

Chocolate icing
Rich and smooth, its level of sweetness depends on the type of chocolate used. Use dark chocolate with no more than 70% cocoa solids or it will be too bitter. Use milk chocolate with at least 30% cocoa solids and use the best quality white chocolate you can find.

225 g/8 oz dark, milk or white chocolate, chopped
75 g/3 oz unsalted butter

Melt the chocolate and butter together in a bowl over a pan of simmering water, stirring until smooth. Use immediately.

Chocolate ganache

Lighter and creamier than chocolate icing, again its sweetness level depends on the chocolate used. See 'Chocolate icing' for information on the type of chocolate to use for best results.

75 ml/6 fl oz double cream or full-fat crème fraîche
250 g/9 oz dark, milk or white chocolate, chopped

Bring the cream to the boil in a small pan, remove from the heat and stir in the chocolate. Leave until the chocolate has melted, then beat with a wooden spoon until smooth. Leave to cool at room temperature, not in the fridge, until thick enough to spread, stirring occasionally, then whisk for 1-2 minutes until light. If the icing becomes too thick, microwave on medium power in 5 second bursts until it returns to the right consistency.

Cream cheese frosting

115 g/4 oz full-fat cream cheese
50 g/2 oz unsalted butter, softened
225 g/8 oz icing sugar

Whisk together the cream cheese, butter and icing sugar until smooth and creamy. Use immediately, or press cling film over the surface to prevent a crust forming and keep refrigerated.

Decorating with chocolate

Have chocolate at room temperature, not too cold, when grating, chopping or making large curls. Use a small, double thickness greaseproof bag for piping chocolate.

Chocolate curls

Melt the chocolate in a small heatproof bowl set over simmering water, then cool for 10 minutes. Spread onto a cold work surface – a slab of marble is ideal. When cold, use a sharp knife almost parallel to the surface and push through the chocolate.

Chocolate shavings

Use a swivel vegetable peeler along the flat side of a large bar of chocolate, shaving it off in curls.

Chocolate leaves

Brush or coat the underside of clean, unblemished rose or bay leaves with melted chocolate, then leave to set. Peel the leaf away from the chocolate. Store the fragile leaves in an airtight container.

Chocolate triangles

Melt chocolate in a small bowl set over simmering water, then cool for 10 minutes. Spread onto a piece of baking parchment and when cold, cut into triangles.

Home-made cupcake cases

If you want to be economical (or individual) you can make your own cases. It is best to use greaseproof paper, waxed paper or baking parchment but you can experiment with brown paper, wrapping paper and doyleys. Line non-culinary use papers with greaseproof as well and avoid any paper with strong coloured dyes or glues as these may melt and seep through into your mixture. Cut out sufficient rounds of paper using a saucer or CD as a template. Find a tumbler or bottle that fits snugly into the cup indentations of your bun or muffin tin. Place a paper circle on top of each cup compartment and push the bottle down to press the paper into the tin and create a paper case. Make sure the papers are neatly creased flat against the cup sides to ensure an even finish. Use 10 cm/4 in squares of paper for a pointed edged case and, if liked, trim the edges with pinking shears.

Recipe index